Your Shift Matters:

Surviving to Thriving

19 Amazing Stories of Hard Times,

Healing and Heroism

Compiled by
Dana Zarcone

For more information, visit:

Compiler / Publisher: www.danazarcone.com

Book and cover design by: Jennifer Insignares www.yourdesignsbyjen.com

Editing by: Amanda Ni Odhrain www.amandahoranediting.com

Formatting by: Bojan Kratofil https://facebook.com/bojan.kratofil

ISBN: 978-1-5136-3120-2

Gratitude

I want to start by showing my appreciation for all the authors of this book who, like myself, have a passion for serving others and making the world a better place. I feel blessed, honored and grateful to have you on this journey with me.

We've come together to share our stories in hopes that it will touch the lives of others and inspire them to live all-in and full-out. To inspire them to make a shift from simply surviving to totally thriving in all aspects of their lives. I know some, if not all of you, are taking a big risk. Maybe you're revealing yourself in a way that's never been shared before, or you're telling a story that's never been told before. Either way, I know that, by sharing your stories, you will touch many hearts and ignite many spirits. Thank you! I hope that this journey has been as amazing for you as it has been for me!

The past few years have been full of some serious ups and downs. Some of which I'm sure I'll write about in future books. For now, suffice it to say I wouldn't be where I am today without so many beautiful friends in my life. People who support me, love me and even give me a swift, well-needed kick in the keister at times. I'm grateful for all that they do!

I'm especially grateful to the friends, mentors and coaches that I've worked with over the years. You have been instrumental in showing me all the amazing ways that I can own my brilliance, help people own theirs and make the world a better place at the same time. Thank you for pushing me and encouraging me to never give up – even though there were times when I wanted to!

In addition, the one person that had a big influence in my life is my mother. She always believed in me, even when I didn't believe in myself. Unfortunately, she has passed now. However, I know that she's still cheering me on from above. Thanks, Mom, for everything! I love you, and I miss you so, so much!

I would be remiss not to include my dad as well. I love you, Dad! Thank you for being there for me and helping to make my dreams come true! I couldn't have done it without you!

Finally, I am so grateful for my husband and two daughters who have sacrificed a lot for me. Thank you all very much for your love and support. To my daughters, I will say that I hope I'm able to inspire you, just as my mom inspired me, to follow your dreams and never give up! And, never forget, *Your Shift Matters!*

Table of Contents

Foreword

I met Dana a few years ago when she was participating in a book that I was co-publishing. We clicked immediately. Dana's tenacity was strong and beautiful because her light comes from within. It is no surprise or coincidence that she is publishing her own books now.

When we desire to shift from surviving to thriving in life, we become more aware of our truest desires, our soulful life, and the place where we are meant to be living. This can be a challenge due to all the distractions and minutia around us. We all need support. Dana's vision and intuition, along with her co-authors, will provide that support. They will show you how to step into the life you are meant to lead – a life where ease, joy, love, and peace comes daily.

This book is a road map of life in your hands. A beautiful shift awaits you.

As I said, it comes as no surprise to me that Dana has become such a great leader. She is a woman that is walking, implementing, and living her talk.

My personal shift occurred at a red light at a busy intersection. I fell asleep in the middle of the day. I had zero reasons to be tired. In fact, I wasn't, I was just completely dead inside. I would wake up and wonder when I could return to bed. I am a highly energetic morning person now, but I wasn't back then. As I was entering my fifties, I knew I wasn't going to make it like this. I was living without passion, barely surviving. I needed to make a huge shift, and fast.

I made phone calls, surrendered, and asked for help – something I wasn't very good at. Asking for help meant I had to admit to others that I was struggling. From the outside, it looked like I had everything together, and I didn't want to shatter that belief that others had in me.

I was missing faith in my life, a higher power to guide me. I began a journey to rediscover my faith in God, my beliefs, and myself.

I believe in a higher power, the energies to help us shift. We are always changing, and we always need support. We can receive it from like-minded individuals, groups, meditation, prayer, and belief.

This book can be your support. Read it in bed at night or when you sit down with a cup of morning coffee to plan your day.

Start thriving. We all believe in you.

Kim Boudreau Smith
Her Bold Voice
www.kimbsmith.com

Introduction

Welcome to the Your Shift Matters book series! A series of books that is sure to inspire, motivate and move you in ways you've never felt before. This series brings authors together from all walks of life who share raw and real stories of overcoming unimaginable challenges, rising strong, and learning many lessons along the way. Their stories are sure to challenge your mind, touch your heart, and ignite your spirit.

When I started my podcast Your Shift Matters, I never thought in a million years that it would lead me down this powerful path of creating a book series. The underlying message in all of my work is that you have to deal with your shit in order to make a shift!

This is something that I'm very passionate about because I've seen and experienced a lot of suffering, as have the authors of this book. I'm certain you've experienced your fair share of suffering as well. This breaks my heart because we suffer needlessly! We aren't meant to suffer. We're supposed to feel vibrantly alive; resonating with love, joy, and compassion. We're meant to live a fulfilling, meaningful life. Yet, the majority of us don't live this way.

In this book, the authors will unveil their suffering to you. They have shared their stories of overcoming adversity, facing tough challenges and shifting from merely surviving in life to completely thriving. They will bring you along on their journey and share the pain, heartbreak, agony, grief, sorrow, and suffering they've endured. Yep! They want you to understand that you're not alone.

Their stories will inspire you and give you hope. They will give you a sense of knowingness that if they can overcome the pain they've had to endure, so can you!

I invite you to read each story without judgment, with an open heart and genuine compassion. By doing so, it's my suspicion that you will find a little bit of yourself in each one. You too will realize that life is not about just surviving, it's about finding happiness and thriving. As you read each of these stories, I hope you feel that you aren't alone in your suffering and that there's nothing to be ashamed of - there's nothing to fear. You've got this!

You see, shame and fear are very close friends, and they will keep you stuck. When you feel ashamed of your struggles, and you're afraid to make a change, you'll struggle to survive. As a result, you will never be able to thrive and step into the person you were born to be.

I'm passionate about this because so many people suffer, stay stuck, and live unhappy lives for no other reason than they refuse to deal with their shit! Are you one of them? I was guilty of this for a very long time. I'm sure my authors have been guilty of this as well. Instead of dealing with the issue - or perhaps more importantly - the pain associated with the issue, everything is swept under the rug or pushed aside in hopes it will all go away; It won't. When it doesn't, we're quick to look outside ourselves for the easy button, happy pill, or magic potion that will make it all better.

Through my education, personal experience and working with hundreds of clients across the globe, I am convinced more than ever that quick fixes aren't sustainable. They won't help you make the life-changing shift that you need. Instead, you have to deal with your shit in order to make a shift, just like the authors of this book have.

Are you ready to thrive?

It's through my podcast, this book and the amazing stories the authors share that you'll find the hope, inspiration, and the determination to do what you need to do to start thriving and loving life!

Remember, at the end of the day, in order to live your life all-in and full-out, Your Shift Matters!

With lots of heartfelt love and gratitude,

Dana Zarcone
The Liberating Leadership Coach.
Coach | Trainer | Best Selling Author | Publisher | Motivational Speaker
www.danazarcone.com

Dana Zarcone

Known as The Liberating Leadership Coach, Dana is passionate about helping her clients live all-in and full-out, step into their power, and enjoy epic success in life and business. Following a successful twenty-four-year corporate career, Dana earned her master's degree in counseling.

She works as a national certified counselor, certified Core Energetics practitioner, certified kinesiologist and leadership coach. Dana provides leadership training as well as individual and group coaching. She's a coach, trainer, motivational speaker, international bestselling author and publisher, and host of the *Your Shift Matters* podcast.

Dana integrates neuroscience, quantum physics, kinesiology, and psychology to show her clients what is truly possible. Through her broad range of education, research, and experience, Dana has developed a novel approach that has helped hundreds of clients make measurable, positive shifts in their lives.

Find Dana online:

Websites: www.DanaZarcone.com
www.YourShiftMatters.com
Twitter: www.Twitter.com/DanaZarcone

Chapter 1

Slaying My Dragons

By Dana Zarcone

Dry toast, broiled chicken, and steamed vegetables were the staples in my diet for the better part of a month at the ripe old age of twelve. My mother took me to the doctor because she thought I was overweight. Her fears were confirmed. The doctor told my mother that I was a 'bit overweight' and should lose 10 lbs to get back on track.

This was good for my mother. She couldn't stand the fact that I was a chubby little kid. I suspect she had her own body image issues. I also think she felt that it reflected on her abilities as a mother. So, the fact that I was overweight was tough for her.

While she would never tell me directly that she was concerned about my weight, she'd find a way to make her point. Many times she'd put her arms around my waist, squeeze my 'love handles' and remind me that "no boy is going to want to feel *that* when they hug you!" She'd also tell me how cute it was that I didn't walk...I waddled!

Clearly, this was one of the reasons I struggled with body image issues most of my life. I now know that these issues started way before her manipulative taunting.

Somewhere along the way, I came to the conclusion that I didn't matter. That I was unlovable, unworthy and insignificant. Growing up I always felt isolated, alone and empty. I suspect that some of it is due to being a middle child and some of it is the result of traumatic experiences I had growing up.

My older brother was less than thrilled when I came along (that's putting it lightly!). By his own admission, he hated me for being born. I can't say I blame him. I'm sure all that negative, resentful energy affected the 'bundle of joy' energy that I had come into this world with. When my parents picked up on his lack of enthusiasm for my arrival, I'm sure they did what all good parents would do. They took extra measures to make sure that he was content, tended too and reassured that he was loved. Several years later, my sister was born. Now I'm the classic middle child vying for attention.

Middle child syndrome is a very real thing! I know this first hand from experience and from my formal education as I earned my masters in counseling. Middle children have to try a lot harder to be heard, get noticed and be seen. We usually have to find creative ways to get our parents attention and, in most cases, we don't succeed. As a result, we begin to believe that they don't care and we start to make up stories about ourselves – limiting beliefs that become etched in our brains.

The beliefs I had - that I didn't matter, that I'm unlovable, unworthy and insignificant - had a deep, profound effect on my confidence and self-esteem growing up. The sad thing is that, for me, nothing could be farther from the truth. My parents loved me very much! I just couldn't see it.

Eventually, I became depressed and turned to food as a way to feel better. The school bus would drop us off in the parking lot at the corner grocery store. Before walking home, I'd go into the store and buy a box of chocolate covered cherries. Yum! I'd get home, swiftly walk to my room and hide them under the bed.

I had the best of intentions. My goal was to eat just one yummy, ooey-gooey, chocolate covered cherry a day. A treat for myself that no one had to know about. Only, I never followed my own rules. By the end of the day, the entire box would be gone. Yep, this sweet treat soothed my soul!

I needed a lot of soothing. Not only did I suffer from the middle child syndrome, I never really fit in with the kids at school either. I was a freckle-faced Irish girl and the kids used to say I had cooties. I remember playing Kiss Tag in 3rd grade. This is a game where a boy would chase after a girl and, if they caught her, they'd get to give her a kiss. A boy was chasing after me and when he caught me he said "Oh gross! Cooties!" and ran away.

I had a similar experience in 8th grade when I was at a party and we were playing Spin the Bottle. This is a game where players sit in a circle, and a bottle is placed in the middle. A player spins the bottle and whoever it points to when it stops spinning gets a kiss.

A very popular, handsome, jock spun the bottle and it landed on me! Wow! My first kiss with someone *like him*! We got up and went around the corner to have some privacy. However, instead of kissing me I heard the most devastating words ever. "I really don't want to kiss you. So, let's not kiss and just *say* we did." I kept my cool and replied "Yeah, I was thinking the same thing! Glad we're on the same page."

Of course, we weren't on the same page! My heart sank deep into the pit of my stomach. I was choking back the tears. I was totally crushed!

What's wrong with me?" I wondered.

In high school, I had very few dates. At that point, I had given up on the idea of ever having a boyfriend so I focused on other things. I immersed myself in sports; playing softball, volleyball, swimming, diving, track and high jump. I discovered that I was a pretty good athlete. I was a four-year letterman in track and came in second place in high jump at the state competition. I wasn't a girlie girl by any means. More of a tom-boy of sorts, so guys thought I was pretty cool. Dates were still few and far between though.

Prom came around and one of my brother's friends was kind enough to take me so I didn't have to miss it. In your face, high school guys! I'm dating a college boy! At least that's what I wanted them to think!

During my senior year, my friends and I discovered the frat parties at the local university. My brother belonged to one but I was given strict orders to stay away from his fraternity and all of his friends. Unfortunately, I didn't obey the rules! I was having too much fun!

Now, I looked forward to Saturday nights because, these college guys – or dare I say 'men' - found me quite attractive. Finally, I was getting noticed and I was receiving some much needed attention!

One guy, in particular, was flirting with me all the time. He made me feel special - like I mattered. He made me feel that I just might be worthy and lovable after all! He asked me out on a date and, of course, I said yes. Only no one could know about it…especially my brother, because he would never approve!

I met him behind the frat house, and we drove to Look Out Point. He brought a bottle of wine with him, which we drank as we admired the gorgeous skyline and city lights below. Eventually, we started making out and things got out of hand. I said 'no'. I said it many times but apparently, in his world, 'no' meant 'yes'. I froze. I didn't know what to do. I thought, *Is this really happening? How could this be happening to me!?*

When I got home, I drew a bath, and soaked in it for hours. I felt dirty. I wanted to scrub every nasty, disgusting germ off my skin! I oscillated between being in total shock and disbelief to feeling completely numb to crying my eyes out. What's so sad about this is that I blamed myself. I wasn't supposed to go to those parties. I wasn't supposed to date a guy in college. It was all my fault! I broke the rules, and this was my penance.

Once again, my beliefs about myself were confirmed. I don't matter, I'm unlovable, and I'm unworthy and insignificant. The important thing to note here is that these beliefs came about because I made them up! Nobody pulled me aside and said, "Hey Dana. I just want you to know that you're unlovable!" These beliefs, albeit deeply ingrained in my psyche, were really assumptions I made because of the experiences I had.

We all have deep-rooted, self-limiting beliefs that ultimately determine whether we have the courage to empower ourselves, or let others define who we are. Experts say that by the time we're seven, we've developed limiting beliefs and negative thought patterns that ultimately determine our reality and becomes our personality!

From the time we're born, we are exposed to attitudes, feelings, and prejudices that we adopt as our own. We are inundated with external stimuli and subliminal messages that wreak havoc on our lives. Ultimately, they contribute to our limiting beliefs and negative patterns of thinking. Your beliefs determine what you think, and how you feel emotionally and physically. This, in turn, dictates what action you take and the results that you get.

The #MeToo movement is a powerful one. This is a movement where people who have been sexually harassed or abused are finally speaking out against the perpetrator after being silent for a very long time, sometimes decades. It's powerful because the victims are finally taking a stand and the perpetrators are being held accountable for their wrong doing. While this movement is giving victims a voice, and the power to speak out, I feel there's more to it.

I believe the flipside of the #MeToo coin is #MyPart. We have to hold ourselves accountable for how we played a part in what happened. Don't get me wrong, this isn't about blaming the victim. And by no means does this excuse the violation or make it right in any way. It's about understanding the dynamics that are at play when we're interacting with people.

Pragmatically, I made choices that put me in that situation. I broke the rules. I went out on a date with someone I wasn't supposed to be with. I didn't listen to my intuition telling me something wasn't right.

From a psychological perspective, I had something to gain by going on that date. Because I felt like I didn't matter, that I was unlovable and insignificant. I was constantly looking for validation outside myself that the opposite was true. My insecurity and low self-esteem meant that I had a need to be seen, liked, and adored.

Looking back, I am certain that this need impacted my choices. When I received a compliment, I soaked it up like a dry sponge. When I was being flirted with, I would flirt back. By going on a date with someone who I thought adored me, I finally felt that I mattered; that I was lovable after all. Even though I said 'no' many times, I craved the attention so much that I put myself in that situation.

What happened to me was unacceptable. His behavior was unconscionable and criminal. However, I knew I couldn't heal or move on while I remained a victim. I had to look at my part and this meant owning that, in a bizarre way, I was using him to feel loved, good enough and worthy.

Looking at my part is important for all areas of my life! If I just sit back, and blame others for all the ways my life sucks, I am powerless. I am merely surviving!

So many of us think of ourselves as nothing more than victims. We go around sighing, "Woe is me. How could they do this to me! It's all their fault. If they didn't do X, then I wouldn't be experiencing Y. Nobody loves me." As victims, we allow ourselves to be ruled, and heavily influenced, by others' actions, judgments and behaviors. Being in a chronic state of victimhood means that I never have to assume responsibility for my part in what happens to me – as if it's always someone else's fault. When I'm in a victim state, I am emotionally dependent and powerless, looking for someone else to fix it. The only one who could fix me was me.

Continually thinking of myself as the victim meant that I was a prisoner of my own unhealed emotions. I had harbored deep, intense feelings of guilt, shame, rage, anger, and resentment. All of which I carried around with me day after day. Oh what a burden!

Eventually, all of this got the better of me. I ended up struggling with depression as an adult. I suffered as a result of all the limiting beliefs I had, the negative chatter in my head and all the emotional pain I buried hoping I wouldn't have to deal with it again. We all do that right? We try to leave the past in the past and just move on with our lives?

Unfortunately, it doesn't work that way.

The past is always in the present. We've all got demons and dragons lurking on the sidelines, quietly wreaking havoc on our lives! Until we find a way to slay the dragons, we're merely surviving, living our lives on auto-pilot, by default, not by design. It's our job to find a way to slay the dragons so that we can thrive again!

When I embarked on my healing journey, I tried everything under the sun! Antidepressants, motivational books, supplements, and talk therapy. None of them worked for me. Why? Because I was looking 'out there' for the solution when I should have been looking within. As the saying goes, you can only go as high as you're willing to go deep. Only, I didn't want to go deep. I was petrified of doing so because I didn't want to relive all the drama and trauma and I certainly didn't want to feel the intense pain I've avoided for so long.

I learned that when you're not willing to go within, you will go without! Without real happiness, without a sense of meaning and purpose, without the possibility of reaching your full potential. You'll continue to suffer needlessly, maybe even endlessly when you don't have to.

It's through my journey of self-discovery that I was able to shift from surviving to thriving. When I was in survival mode, I was living in the past. I was sitting on the sidelines waiting for someone to come along and give me a ride. I was willing to hitch a ride with someone else in the driver's seat and go in the direction they wanted to take me.

In order to start thriving, I had to whip out my own roadmap, start charting my own course and head in a direction that would allow me to be the powerful, confident, vibrant woman I was born to be. To free myself from all of the emotional and mental debris that's littered my world and prevented me from standing in my greatness.

The way I saw it was that I had two choices. The first was to lie down, maintain the victim mindset and fall deep into the abyss. The second was to stand tall, own my part, and find the courage to do the work I needed to do to heal. To choose to fight for my rightful place on this planet!

I chose to fight! (I am Irish after all.)

In order to shift from surviving to thriving I had to identify and transform the limiting beliefs that were governing my choices, actions and behavior. What beliefs did I have ingrained in my subconscious mind that were impacting how I saw myself, others and the world around me? Were they true, or something I made up?

I also had to listen intently to all of the negative chatter in my head. That little voice that speaks from a place of fear, telling me all the reasons why I can't, won't or shouldn't take a risk in life. What were these toxic thoughts that haunted me? Some were 'I'll never be accepted for who I am.' 'I'll never be loved unless I'm thin.' 'They'll never take me seriously.' Once I became aware of this toxic, negative chatter, I was able to acknowledge it, recognize when it showed up and neutralize it.

Finally, I had to deal with all the pain that I had buried so long ago! What emotions did I still harbor that were keeping me stuck? Believe me, there were a lot of them!

Through my experience and extensive education, I've learned that our beliefs, thoughts and emotions are all energy. We are all energy. So to transform your life you need to transform your energy.

How do you transform your energy so you can shift from simply surviving to ultimately thriving? The bottom line is that you have to deal with your shit in order to make a shift! (Hence my brand, Your Shift Matters!)

Contrary to what we'd like to believe, there aren't any easy buttons or happy pill solutions. Sure, they may bring some relief and take the edge off but they aren't sustainable. In the end, they don't resolve the overarching issues that stem from our beliefs, thoughts and feelings.

To shift from surviving to thriving, I've developed a four-step formula that I use with my clients. Get Real – Reveal – Deal - Heal.

Get Real: As the saying goes, you can't change what you don't acknowledge. If you're not happy or fulfilled in any area of your life, be honest with yourself and admit it.

Reveal: Identify why things aren't working for you. What drama or trauma needs to be healed? How do you really feel about yourself? What limiting beliefs and negative thoughts need to be discovered and transformed? What emotional wounds need to be addressed once and for all?

Deal: Once you can admit that your life isn't working the way you want it to and you've identified some of the root causes, it's time to deal with it. It's time to slay the dragons. Face them head on and process through it so they can be neutralized and cleared.

Heal: The healing stage is less about fixing yourself than it is a practice of letting go. During the healing process, you're able to release blocks and change behaviors that limit you mentally, emotionally, physically and spiritually.

During the healing process, you'll receive clarity and insight about your life path. Healing promotes a deeper connection with your true, authentic self. It helps you experience greater peace, balance and freedom. It is also instrumental in helping you live your true potential.

By going through these four steps, by owning your part as a conscious co-creator, you can shift from simply surviving to totally thriving!

Heather Andrews

Lifestyle strategist, certified Follow It Thru health coach and international bestselling author, Heather Andrews initially created the inspiring Mom on the Go change mentorship program in a bold, immediate response to being 'restructured' out of her 'dream' management position in the beleaguered healthcare system.

Heather's veritable 'rediscovery' of her self-esteem, and her journey to the realization of a deeper, personal led her to ultimately embrace entrepreneurship wholeheartedly. With her own publishing company, and bestseller based on her signature story, Obstacles Equal Opportunities, as well as a foray into podcasting and internet radio, where she will host her own show, Follow It Thru to a Stellar Life.

A voice for self-discovery and fearless revitalization, she is making a positive difference.

Find Heather online:

Websites: www.followitthru.com
            www.heatherandrews.press
Facebook: www.facebook.com/followitthru

Chapter 2

The Priceless Value of Self-Worth

By Heather Andrews

In the wise words of Eleanor Roosevelt, 'No one can make you feel inferior without your consent.'

If I had known then what I know now about my issues with self-worth, it would have made a *huge* difference to my life and my world. Especially on that pivotal day of personal upheaval that is etched in my mind forever.

I was leading a staff meeting when my 'spidey senses' started tingling. Human Resources needed to speak with me on the phone. Intuitively, I just knew that my twelve years of devoted service, including the last three in my dream management role, was all over. A job for which I had sacrificed my health, my family and, my sanity.

It was confirmed, I was restructured out. I have the gift of gab, but that day rendered me speechless. *How could this happen,* I asked myself over and over again. I was unemployed for the first time ever.

I knew that organizations restructured all the time, but that didn't stop the flood of feelings. Shame, unworthiness, and of course, rejection.

My old childhood friend, *rejection*. The same emotion I struggled so hard to overcome. I thought I had worked so diligently on my personal growth for years to get beyond all this!

I was a brilliant manager, an amazing mom to my three teenagers, and a good wife. I was strong and self-confident – a highly esteemed powerhouse of a modern woman. Yet, in one awful minute, *boom*, I was dragged back in time to my childhood and that feeling of unworthiness.

In my mind, I had clearly 'failed', so I was a 'failure', and, rational or not, I felt so ashamed. We've all been there, haven't we?

How is it we can be so high on 'happy', ruling the world one minute, and then plunged into despair the next, drowning in unworthiness?

I went into survival mode; angry, blaming and having a pity party for several months, until I realized that was my own perception. I was triggered by old emotions from my childhood, where I was taught to believe you needed to be thin to be loved. I was fat. This carried on into my school years. I never felt accepted because I did not accept myself. It carried on into my university years, where I met my first husband.

I learned low self-worth, and lack of self-confidence can come from our early years through dysfunction and lack of love. It shows up in the choices we make as adults through financial trouble, broken relationships, and how we let ourselves be treated by others. It's a constant battle to keep our heads *and* self-worth above water when life batters us with its constant storms. It can hinder us until we learn and establish our own sense of value and self-worth.

I knew that fateful day when I lost my dream job was obviously an obstacle. Fed up with the obsolete patterns in my life, I was determined to turn this situation into an opportunity, a chance to make a profound change. I never wanted to go through that crazy instability of false highs and self-hating lows again.

In other words, our own sense of deserving, of worthiness, our estimation of self…it is all under *our* control. Each individual can make a choice of how he or she feels about themselves. We may know this, but we may not understand how to achieve it. My self-worth is about my relationship with me.

Our internal value is a priceless commodity. Positive self-worth and self-love is the foundation each of us needs to build whatever we want in life. Without it, the pretty castle will come crashing down the minute someone or something from the outside pushes our emotional buttons, causing us to self-sabotage and emotionally implode.

A fulfilling career, functional and caring relationships with friends and loved ones, health, wealth, abundance, or anything else we desire, starts with knowing that we *deserve* the good. We should not deprive ourselves because we feel like we 'failed', and therefore, 'bad' in someone else's estimation.

Failure is a part of learning and growing as a human being. Just because you 'fail', it does not mean you're a 'failure'. None of us are perfect, and that's ok.

I remember how I spoke to myself in years gone as I looked in the mirror. *If only I could lose 20 lbs. Then someone will love me. Then I will be ok.* I did not accept myself for who I was – the magical essence of me. I am my own why, and you are yours.

My view of not being enough could have affected my children, whose inquiring eyes watched my every move as their role model. Kids base their belief systems on how they are raised, and it affects future generations.

My lack of self-worth began to affect how I cared for myself. I found many excuses not to exercise. I ate crappy food and drank a ton of wine.

I blamed everyone and everything for my circumstances. My own huge pity party.

It took me back to my first marriage, which was far from Stellar.

I see now that this situation happened because of my own intrinsic lack of self-worth. I now realize that I created this unhappy scenario myself. I could have left him. I eventually did, but at the time, being relatively unenlightened, I stayed in the less than par relationship because I didn't believe anyone else would love me. Even that half-life was better than being alone. Even though we have long since divorced, when I think about what I endured and why, I still get goose bumps down my spine.

Someone I regarded very highly asked me, quite bluntly, "Do you love yourself?" *Huh?* I was twenty-three years old and barely knew what that meant.

This seemingly simple question touched off a profound mission of self-discovery when I realized that, surprisingly, my answer was "no".

Even though I was confident and competent in my career, I saw that I was using it as an avoidance technique. I kept myself so busy that I didn't have to face up to my issues of low self-worth. Although it seemed like I had it all together, clearly, I did not love myself enough to choose a more positive, satisfying relationship.

I did not treat my body well. I failed to respect my hard-earned money, frittering it away on 'retail therapy' in the hope that it would fill my empty soul.

All of the triggers came back to me on that fateful day when I lost my job. It took me down a very dark and lonely path for about a year, bringing back on the pain that I thought I had dealt with.

Each day seemed to bring a new shift, a memory, or a lesson learned. I hired coaches to help me work through each step. I went to courses and transformation weekends and each time I came out a bit more hopeful that maybe I would find Heather again.

It was in the spring and fall of 2017 that I attended three seminars that truly changed my life. I learned that I was over-analyzing everything in my head. My heart was so empty; I could not feel love nor did I trust anyone enough to allow them to get close to me. I deflected and talked about what I was doing versus who I was being. I realized I was so closed off that I could not have any close relationships. I did not see myself as worthy.

That weekend I accepted the honesty of others. I was promised that it was a safe place to open up. We had been teamed up with a buddy and once I realized how much anger, shame, and fault I felt, tears came flooding to the surface. This buddy of mine held my hand and offered me a Kleenex.

Many tears were shed; it was a turning point to let the floodgates open. What happened that day left me raw, but I also found my heart. I still had a long way to go, but I had turned a corner, and there were people there holding lanterns, so to speak, to share their light with me.

I learned many lessons during my time there.

I was living my actions of 'yesterday' that day. I had to break the cycle of yesterday and know that just because I was in one place did not mean I had to stay there.

As one of the forerunners of the whole self-help movement, Dr. Maxwell Maltz was known to say, "Low self-esteem is like driving through life with your handbrake on." I can finally say that losing my dream job turned out to be the catalyst that spurred me on to a much deeper understanding of myself. It opened up so many new avenues for me that I would not have discovered otherwise. I knew I could not go back and start over, but I discovered that I could move forward towards a different story with an outstanding ending.

We can never change the past, but we can learn from it. We can't control what's happening around us, or the obstacles we meet in life, but we can control the way we react to them. It's a choice, sink or swim. Get pulled down into the depths of undeserving worthlessness, or trust in that unique, indestructible essence of YOU. Become the divine creator of your destiny!

See yourself as a beloved friend, and speak to yourself accordingly, with kindness and respect. Work towards self-acceptance. You're not perfect, and never will be, but that's more than ok.

Don't judge your 'insides' by everyone else's 'outsides'. You have no idea what's behind the façade of other people's lives. We are all on our own path, so keep focused on moving forward on your own journey.

Tony Robbins said, "You always get out of life exactly what you tolerate." So stop settling and start believing!

Believe that you deserve the very best. Then go out there and get it! The result of believing in your self-worth will affect all areas of your life. You will be more accountable and hold yourself to a higher standard. This, in turn, will create ripples in every area of your life.

One tool I used when I was moving through my shift of discovering me was the four R's.

Realize: I became aware of how I really felt. I had to meet myself and get real.

Reset: I had to reset my thinking and my reactions.

Reframe: I began to look at my life through a new lens. Look at your situation with curiosity. It is the most powerful tool we have. Ask yourself, *I wonder what would happen if I felt this way or I did it this way?* That was a game changer.

Resiliency: I know that I choose how I react. I learned to have a plan B and roll with what is happening. I have the power to bounce back or bounce in.

When we shine our light, it gives permission for others to shine their light. Sometimes we need to get out our shovel and dig deep within ourselves to find it.

I am so lucky, so blessed to have come to understand that I am the creator of my life. I deserve the best. I want it all, and I want it delivered, as it says on my wise fridge magnet.

Never in a million years did I think I would become the inspirational speaker, writer, and publisher that I am today. The difference is, now, I believe in me.

I am a brilliant woman.

I am a great mother.

I am a loving wife.

I am passionate.

I am committed.

I am worthy.

I am deserving.

Now, I mentor others to help them understand that they can feel the same way.

Imagine if we all came from a healthy place of confident self-worth, and the understanding that we are all responsible for creating our own reality. Just imagine the difference that would make in our world.

Come with me, it is better over here.

Monica Armstrong

Monica is a spiritual mentor who offers support to women undernourished by faith traditions that neglect women's unique spiritual needs. Combining spirituality and creativity, she guides and nurtures the soul with the wisdom of Sophia, the feminine divine, who is 'hidden in plain sight' in scripture. Developing creativity and connectedness to the divine within increases resiliency and the capacity for love and forgiveness. The inner movement from fear to faith brings clarity to the meaning and purpose of their life's journey.

Founder of Spirit Matters Studio, Monica is an artist and educator, holding graduate certifications in holistic spirituality and spiritual direction.

Find Monica online:

Website: www.MonicaArmstrong.com
Facebook: Spirit Matters Studio
Instagram: armstrong1691

Chapter 3

The Worst Best Day of My Life

By Monica Armstrong

The worst day of my life – was it the day I was diagnosed with cancer? No. Was it the day I watched my husband disappearing as he walked away, ending our marriage? No again. Worse than those horrible moments was the day I received the news that my five year-old son had a brain injury. I was devastated, rigid with panic. I looked into the abyss of uncertainty, fear and the surrender of all the hopes and dreams I had for my sweet little boy.

A visual artist, I had recently completed a massive public mural commission and returned to creating my own work in my studio. My life looked good from the outside: a nice home in the suburbs, a husband and son, a great studio and finally, the emergence of some professional success. But I was miserable. My partner often worked nights, holed up in his home office during the day, using 'important' phone calls and naps on the couch to avoid engagement in our lives. I felt isolated and frustrated by this man who popped in and out of our lives and our home as if it was a hotel and I was the concierge. My patience with my husband's inability to stick to a job was exhausting. Despite his advanced degrees, he was in sales, changing every few months, always on commission, investing our limited funds in chancy business ventures. Our connection to each other was shriveling. I was lonely and scared by his secretive behavior. Our finances were a nightmare. A good night's sleep was a rarity.

Twenty years of struggle as an artist was finally bringing my work recognition. My work was maturing, attaining representation in galleries. I was exhibiting nationally and had commissions, but I was at the end of my rope with my marriage. We were ten years in and there was little to no physical, emotional, intellectual relationship or social life. When he didn't show up for his son's birthday party, held at home while he hid in his home office, I snapped. "Choose a lawyer or a therapist," I stated through clenched teeth. "I cannot go on like this." Ironically, our first counseling appointment was on Valentine's Day. When we returned home from a rather discouraging session, there was a phone message waiting that turned my life upside down.

For months, our son had been having problems at home and school, tripping and falling easily, losing former abilities such as tying shoes, reading, and writing. He had become easily frustrated and tearful. Increasingly, he seemed incapable of following simple instructions. I didn't know this was happening at school and thought it occurred at home because of the tension between his dad and me.

A frightening teacher conference made me realize there was a real problem. I embarked on a series of discouraging visits to various doctors and specialists. We left each doc with nothing but another referral. There was talk of lowering expectations for him, special schools, and questionable medications for behavior. Finally, I called a relative who worked with children to ask him for a referral to a specialist. He arranged for my son to have a workup by the director of the Family Hope Center. That was what I needed – hope! There they develop unique individualized programs that guide parents through daily intensive therapeutic neurological stimulation to support the children's healing and brain development.

From this workup, the truth finally emerged. The difficulties all stemmed from his premature birth, and the consequences of being in an incubator with the oxygen set too high. This was affecting his vision, hearing, mobility, respiration, and therefore, his understanding. The diagnosis scared me out of my wits.

Terrible scenarios arose in my mind. I could hardly breathe from the fear and pain. Having had plenty of losses and challenges at that point in my life, I thought I knew how to pray. I regularly read books on spirituality and was a churchgoer. However, when my chubby cheeked, curly-headed little boy's future was threatened, my faith was really put to the test. My prayers for him felt like marbles in my mouth. Nothing would come out but fear and tears. I pled, I begged, I demanded, I bargained. I felt desperate and heartbroken. I was both frozen inside and dying of thirst for some relief from my fear for him. I felt I was a terrible mother who should have somehow protected him.

Because of our finances, I was granted a scholarship, enabling me to take the training that would prepare me to begin the therapeutic plan. It was inspiring, enlightening and totally overwhelming. To put this program into action meant pulling my son from school. This was an extremely demanding physical and neurological program, and now I would have homeschooling duties to deal with too. I knew it would fall entirely on my shoulders. This program was all day, every day, with responsibility for creating new materials for the next day. Could I do this?

It was one of the most painful decisions of my life, to choose between his future vs. fruition of twenty years of my work and dreams. Curled up on the couch in my beloved studio, tears and temper tantrums wracked my body and soul. In the end, there was no contest – he won hands down. A week after the training I shut the door of the studio and walked away into the unknown.

The confinement every day, all day, adding up to years was very hard. No artwork, no social life, the tight structure of the daily goals, every minute timed, went against my years of effort to achieve and sustain creative flow. Trying to motivate – not bully – a child into doing repetitive and incomprehensible tasks day after day was horrible. I was so down in myself because of my own irritability. The stakes were so high – I couldn't give up. Multiple times a day I escaped to the basement to 'check the laundry'. Each time I was on the brink of flipping out with impatience, frustration, and fear. Nestled by the washer and dryer sat a rocking chair, a candle, and a prayer book. I'd frantically rock and pray for a few minutes 'to do no harm', to do what was required for him and for me to stay sane. I found myself turning towards a mothering image of the Divine, one who would do anything for her child.

It was during the early period, when I was subject to waves of fear for him and grief for myself that I really learned to pray. I didn't pray with words or my mind, but by FLINGING myself into Her merciful arms. All I had to offer was an open heart and soul, and a fierce willingness to do all that I could so that he would be healed. I opened myself to receiving gifts of strength and patience. I prayed that whatever I experienced during that time would leave no regrets and somehow nourish my artwork someday.

These moments brought me back to the reality of my *gratitude* for hope and the gift it was that I could actually *do* something. This reset enabled me to pull myself together and return to our tiny team of two and our Olympian endeavor.

Meanwhile, I was crushed that his dad spent so little time with our boy. He avoided involvement with the program as much as possible. We argued, promises were made and then broken over and over. I was getting a lesson in the futility of changing or controlling another person.

Our dire finances only added to the stress. He had borrowed so much on the house that there was no equity left. Our credit cards were maxed out and there was little to no income from his neglected sales and impulsive investment schemes. Eventually, we lost our home. I took over the management of our bills, found us an apartment nearer to the clinic, and convinced the landlord that we were trustworthy. I even asked him if we could pay the rent weekly for a while. I was a maniac, working sixteen hours a day on the program, six days a week.

Gradually, those basement prayers grew peace within me. They allowed me to gain such respect for my child's hard work. He crept and crawled, ran and swam, biked and brachiated a thousand miles in his four years of rehabilitation. We accomplished so much together. Imagine being awed daily by your child (even while being aggravated). It was the beginning of my practice of continually reconnecting to Spirit throughout the day, not to beg, but to rest within. It became my joy to create interesting materials for his homeschooling, to be with him so much and able to see improvement …a total blessing. It was also a gift to be able to meet so many other parents and kids who often faced far greater problems. I could clearly see that love was the foundation, the fuel for these Herculean efforts from both the parents and children. It was truly a labor of love that birthed miracles.

I continued supporting my son's program, which now involved a special school and the continuation of intense physical training. Working there full-time to cover the tuition was a new form of torment for me. Initially, because his auditory issue was the last to be resolved, I was required to squish myself into a tiny student desk so that I could then help him with his homework. The things we do for love.

Another year passed, reaping great improvements. He was thriving, but I was only surviving. Longing deeply to get back to my own work, I began to pray for some time to myself asking for a clear sign that he was ready to move on. I didn't want to quit because of my needs, but because he was ready. I started waking up in the middle of the night, unable to sleep. I was so exhausted. I asked, hollered actually, "God! Why are you torturing me?" Of course, eventually, I realized I was getting exactly what I asked for – time alone. In reality, my only opening was the middle of the night. I stopped fighting it. I began to sit in the living room with a lit candle and an open heart – waiting and listening. Within a short time, I had a profound experience, a vision. I will not describe it here, but I will tell you this, it awed, comforted and assured me that we were ready to go back to the world. From this vision came a very large painting called 'Transformation'. It is a mysterious image of one who is rooted in faith, wings spread, encircled by divine energy. Uncertainty melted, I was filled with joy and confidence that all would be well.

This divine message changed my life again. I had no art materials or studio at that time, everything was packed away in boxes. I made a small charcoal drawing from that vision and it was my beacon for the next three months. That's how long it took to transition him back to school and for me to find a new studio. Picking up my brushes after a four-year absence should have been awkward. However, I barely had my coat off before I launched into that huge canvas. Ecstasy! It was followed by a series of twenty paintings called 'The Long Night of the Soul', reflecting on faith and patience. More bodies of work flowed. Those paintings led people to me who encouraged me to begin spiritual direction for myself. That then drew me to graduate studies and a certification in holistic spirituality. Those studies were a fount of inspiration for new art, weaving prayer and meditation into all my work.

My son grew, thrived and became independent, eventually entering college. His dad became quite successful, starting his own financial business. With therapy, we had reached detente at home, following our own pursuits but relatively peaceful.

Then the way opened for me to complete a two-year training to become a spiritual director. Much of the studies were grounded in a contemplative, mystical tradition, emphasizing awareness and the experience of divine presence. It was right up my alley, absolutely coherent with my experience of making art. *It's coming together at last*, I thought.

Ha! A month short of finishing my certification I was diagnosed with cancer. I had been having dreams for a few months that always ended with the phrase, 'You are going to die alone'. Once again, my marriage was breaking down. I thought that was the point of the dream – unaware that cancer was growing within. It was the last straw for my husband of twenty-eight years. He departed, and with him went everything material, financial, and social. I was deeply shocked that I was abandoned at my most vulnerable moment, but this time, in crisis, I had a different foundation – my intact spiritual connection. I knew I was not alone and would never be truly abandoned. I'm a little lop-sided now, but I survived. The ongoing practice of connecting to God, the divine, and to Spirit throughout the day has changed my perspective and abilities in crisis.

Today, I thrive. I own my home and my Spirit Matters Studio. As a mentor, I help people on their spiritual journeys. By focusing on the abundant gifts of the under-recognized feminine divine, I facilitate creativity and spirituality workshops for women. I have also started creating new artwork again. Looking back, I'm grateful for the best worst day of my life, because from that day grew healing for both my son and me, and a transformed future, rooted in love and spirit.

When facing a terrifying event or decision, there are several ways to shift your fearful thoughts and gain access to your spiritual strength:

- Establish a quiet place just for this practice. Sit, resting and let go of words. The Eternal One is as near as your next breath, so BREATHE. When fearful thoughts occur, release them. Know that they are *not true.* Remember, our fears are about things that have not happened yet, therefore they are also not true. Replace each negative thought that arises with a vision of your positive desire.

- Call for help! There are hundreds of names for the divine, use anyone that feels right: Mother, Father, Higher Power, Spirit, Beloved, Jesus, Big Guy, Creator, and more!

- Imagine this presence sitting across the kitchen table with you, a trusted friend. Have a conversation. Expect understanding – not judgment. Allow yourself to become quiet and listen to guidance. Feel for its truth in your heart and gut.

- Practice forgiving yourself first, then others. Forgiveness will lighten your burden, clear your mind, and give you access to more energy to handle your challenge.

- Seek opportunities for gratitude. In most 'bad' situations, there is something 'good'. Gratitude can open the door to potential. Attitude is a powerful transformer.

Blessings!

Dr. Kody Au

Dr. Kody wants to live in a world where the 'why' of every physical injury is found, the true need of every client is uncovered, and individuals are empowered to take control of their injuries.

Following an injury as a registered nurse, Kody obtained his Masters of Science in Exercise and Sports Sciences and a Doctor of Chiropractic graduating with Magna Cum Laude honors.

Kody offers a holistic approach incorporating valuable allopathic experience as a nurse, combined with conservative care treatments to aid individuals with understanding their conditions and empowering them to take control of their injuries and life.

Find Dr. Kody online:

Website: www.baselinewellness.ca
Facebook: www.facebook.com/baselinechiro
Instagram: https://www.instagram.com/baselinechirowellness/

Chapter 4

The Mirror that Changed my Life

By Dr. Kody Au

"I hate him. Why does he look so weird? Why are his eyes so small?" These were phrases that I wholeheartedly embraced as I looked into the mirror every day.

My story takes place in a small town in Saskatchewan known as Meadow Lake. At the time, there was one A&W, one strip mall, and two Chinese restaurants; one of which belonged to my family. I lived with my younger sister, my stay-at-home mother, and my father, who worked extremely hard to provide for us. My family owned The Golden Spur, which consisted of a family restaurant, a bar, and a motel. Many happy memories were created there.

It never dawned on me that I was different. I knew I spoke a different language with my family. I knew I used chopsticks more often than forks and knives, but no one ever treated me differently.

Sadly, children can be cruel. In kindergarten, I was the first Asian student to enter the school system where the population was predominantly Caucasian and Aboriginal. I was asked, "Why are your eyes so small? Why do you look different? What weird food do you have today?" These statements started on day one of school and kept playing in the back of my mind over and over again well into adulthood.

I remember there was a point in time I was afraid to attend school because people would throw rocks at me. There were so many ways that my mom could have dealt with this case. She could have easily brushed my issue aside by telling me to avoid this person, or she could have picked me up each day from school. Instead, she did the best thing possible. Mom emotionally supported me at a time that I felt helpless, and she empowered me by making me feel heard and valued. She stood up for me by talking to the bullies' parents as well as the principal, even though her English was not very proficient. She was the reason that I was no longer bullied. My mom is my hero. She gave me self-worth at a time when I was most vulnerable. This single incident actually brought out the reason why, at a young age, I already wanted to become a doctor. I felt like my calling was to comfort and help others who are experiencing pain.

This was the first point in my life when I realized what others thought about me did not matter. I used all my terrible experiences as fuel to motivate myself to be better. Instead of letting all the negativity and comments drag me down, it made me work harder. I excelled at school, at sports, and in all areas of my life, because I wanted to prove to everyone that yes, I was different, but that I was *worth* it.

The transition from surviving to thriving, no matter how hard I wished, did not happen overnight. I earnestly believe that it is related to all aspects of life. Mentally, I survived my childhood and adolescence, but I did not have a healthy balance. The mindset I developed as a child became a part of me. I developed into an ambitious over-achiever, and I only pushed myself to thrive academically. When I entered the University of Alberta in Edmonton, I realized that consistently pushing did not mean I was thriving. I ended up neglecting everything else in my life. My undergraduate experience opened up the importance of social interactions and made me realize how important it was to foster a balance in my life. It took me a while to warm up, but I ended up meeting some amazing people during my undergraduate experience.

I originally chose to enter into a nursing program as a stepping-stone towards my end goal of becoming a medical doctor. The more I was immersed in the hospital and nursing settings the more I enjoyed it. I was on the front line, working directly with patients. I listened to their stories, their joys, and their sorrows. It was such a blessing to be able to share such special and brief moments in their lives.

After undergrad, I returned to Vancouver and worked as a registered nurse in the Stroke and Medicine Ward at Burnaby Hospital. This was how life is supposed to be, isn't it? I found a good career that paid well and I loved helping people, so this was perfect, right? Wrong!

There were many things I loved about being a nurse. Seeing patients stabilize and go home was the most rewarding part of the profession, although it seldom occurred. These positives also came along with some overwhelming challenges that slowly wore me down. The shift work was difficult mentally and physically, and the stress of having lives in my hands was unrelenting. The unspoken burden of handling the death of patients weighed heavy on my mental health. I often had to force myself to push the sadness aside, since tomorrow was another day.

The bridging position between doctor and patient as a nurse can be a good system. However, one instance made me realize how broken the system really was, and how I was suffering within it.

The situation began with a patient who was demented and dysphagic (unable to swallow). Because of her high risk of choking, we consulted a dietician. Their recommendation was to insert a feeding tube to decrease the risk of choking and pneumonia if fed by mouth. In this specific case, the patient's daughter was adamant that her mother was able to eat and that she would eat if she were fed. After multiple attempts at feeding and several experiences of suctioning this patient when she choked, the nurses advocated inserting a feeding tube for both comfort and safety. The daughter was uncooperative and did not consent to having her mother fed through a tube and instead demanded that the doctor prescribe consistent feeding for her mother. Unfortunately, in this case, the doctor sided with the family instead of the nursing staff and wrote this order against all professional recommendations. As a result, I was the nurse that was caught in the middle of this situation.

I followed the doctor's orders to feed this patient, unknowing that she was at such a high choking risk. I had to suction her three times that morning after observing her choking and decided to consult the doctor about the situation. He was unhelpful and ordered me to continue feeding as per his instructions. As a result, the conflict of doing the patient more harm by following the doctor's orders increased my stress greatly. It was difficult to breathe because of the anxiety I felt from the moral dilemma of doing harm to a patient. After much battling with the doctor, I had to go to the unit manager to state that I was not going to perform a procedure that I felt was unethical. There were threats upon my job, but I had to advocate for my patient's wellbeing.

In the end, the patient ended up getting a feeding tube because the choking risk was too great and the current approach of constant feeding was impossible to continue. The best outcome was provided for the patient, but this event left such a scar that I started looking for other ways to help people. I knew I could no longer continue being the bridge between patient and doctor.

My Search

All aspirations of becoming a medical doctor were crushed, but the universe provides different ways of letting you know what you need to do. While I was soul searching and looking for another way to fulfill my purpose, lightning struck. During the shift, we were understaffed and overcapacity on the unit. I took on a hallway patient who was 6 ft tall and 230 lbs. He was an emergency room overflow patient because he had an extremely low platelet count; this meant that if he started bleeding it would never stop.

On this chaotic day, I ended up saving the man's life three times by catching him as he fell, since he would easily have bled internally if he had hit the floor. After his third fall, I hurt my back so dramatically that I could not finish my shift. I could barely stand up and walking was a challenge. I was twenty-one, with a back injury. I panicked and had no clue of what to do. A colleague of mine luckily saw me and told me to see a chiropractor. This was an event that changed my life forever.

Unable to work, I made an appointment to have my lower back assessed; I had no other choice. After a few visits, I was back at work. This experience was the epiphany that I needed. The universe spoke and gave me a new direction in which I could help people, have a family, and still honor myself. Shortly after, I applied to the University of Western States in Portland, Oregon.

After a vigorous multi-essay application and an interview at the school, I was accepted. I had to pack up everything, move down to Portland, and endure a long distance relationship with my girlfriend back in Vancouver.

I worked hard because my future clients deserved it and I knew that it was the only way that I would be confident in my abilities. Chiropractic school was challenging, our class started with one-hundred and twenty-five students. Sixty graduated.

My dream of helping others was so vivid that it kept me pushing forward. While many students would enjoy their lunch hours off, hang out with other classmates, or explore the city on weekends, I spent most of my time studying or practicing my abilities. I sacrificed a lot of my life during these three years.

My pursuit of excellence pushed me to go even further with my studies. I enrolled in a Masters in Exercise and Sports Sciences program to fill in the gaps that I felt the chiropractic program lacked. The master's program allowed for more experience and detailed education about sports rehabilitation as well as treatment and diagnosis of all the extremities (arms and legs). I finished my clinical hours early and graduated with a Magna Cum Laude honors at the end of the program.

When I returned to Vancouver, life seemed to be moving in the right direction! I had an internship lined up with my mentor, and I passed all my licensing exams. During this time, I was able to observe, build rapport, and improve my abilities further. My mentor is a traditional style of chiropractor, whose primary treatment tool is to adjust the spine. I wanted to be just like him and wanted to mimic his methods.

Six months into my practice, I realized I was suffering once again and that the copycat method that I tried was not for me. I was not happy because I did not feel involved enough with my clients. I felt that I was unable to incorporate what I loved about nursing into my practice. On top of that, I was scared to change because I did not want my mentor to be disappointed in me. It was during this time that unsupportive comments from my childhood began interjecting into my mind. Thoughts of inadequacy, questions about my self-worth and internal turmoil took over and I became lost in my mind. These thoughts and fears kept playing in my mind and my anxiety grew with each day as I continued working.

Thankfully, through the help of a friend, I enrolled in a professional coaching program that changed my mindset on my purpose, vision, and mission. This program was extremely supportive because it addressed my negative childhood thought patterns. It also reinforced and re-inspired my reasons for becoming a healthcare professional in the first place. It gave me tools to work through my challenges and frame them with less of an emphasis on success and failure, and to see them as learning experiences. Additionally, this program made me realize that I was not alone on this journey of entrepreneurship and being a professional. It is very common to have unsupportive stories from the past plague the mind, especially when challenges arise. I learned that what makes a business successful are the systems and the value of the product, which I knew I was not giving to my clients.

My Path

Healthcare and business actually oppose one another. After attending the coaching program, I decided to make the hard decision to change my business model. I chose to focus on the ethics of healthcare instead of those of business. Instead of providing ten-minute treatments consisting of chiropractic manipulations (the industry standard), I decided to provide longer treatments. Overnight, my visits became thirty minutes long and incorporated aspects that I was missing before. Now I included muscle work as well as active rehabilitation exercises to provide a full package care model. This allowed my clients to be empowered to take on their injuries and to be able to rely more on themselves to heal.

At first, I was terrified; I lost some clients that just did not fit the model. The unsupportive thoughts of worthlessness arose again, but I pushed through.

Within a month, things started to pick up. My clients began referring more and more of their friends and families. My business picked up, and within six months, it grew to the point that I had to further advance the style of my practice.

My journey of self-discovery brings me to my current situation. I started my own clinic six months ago, taking a huge leap and starting out on my own. I hired staff to assist me in achieving my vision of helping patients regain control of their physical injuries and their lives. We now have a kinesiologist, a physiotherapist and another chiropractor that shares my vision to help clients for the future. We will take the world of physical medicine by storm. Am I scared of what the future may bring? Deathly afraid. Do I regret my decisions? Not at all.

Throughout all of the challenges of becoming a practitioner and a business owner, I have come to the realization that fear is simply a perception. It is a story of uncertainty and collection of unsupportive stories of the past. Fear itself comes from the unknown and the future. However, they are unpredictable, so why worry. My story is a story of self-acceptance. We all have stories and baggage that we carry with us through life, but the most important part is what meaning you give that baggage. So the next time you look in the mirror and see all of the imperfections and all the things you hate about yourself, think of where these unsupportive thoughts came from. Acknowledge these thoughts, but do not let it be them continue to define who you are. Your story is what makes you unique, so embrace your past and all of those stories, and let them be the fuel source of your future success.

Lacraica Barritt

Following a twenty-five-year career in the automotive industry, Lacraica Barritt decided to go into the insurance industry. Serving clients across the Midwest for over thirteen years, she now owns a very successful insurance company. She is a leader in the industry and enjoys working with her clients.

She is passionate about helping others and does a great deal for her community, including providing supplies for the homeless.

Lacraica is a wine connoisseur, enjoying wines from different regions as she travels around the world. She is well known for her love of dogs and enjoys spending time with her Rottweiler, Kash. She is an avid writer (currently working on her own book), as well as an accomplished artist.

Chapter 5

Faith: It's Not Just Believing, It's Knowing

By Lacraica Barritt

My life has been filled with the usual suspects. The ups, the downs, the good, the bad, and dear Lord – the ugly. I hope that by sharing my story it will help you in some way, and lead you to your 'aha' moment.

I have always been a very spiritual person. Thirty-seven years ago, after attending the Unity Church, I realized that I must be grateful and thankful for everything, (even the bad and the ugly). In those thirty-seven years, I have written TYG (thank you God) in the memo of all my checks. It was a reminder to be thankful. Even on the rocky paths I chose, I was still grateful to breathe, see, walk, and hear…you get the idea. It was a great habit to adopt, and I will continue to do this as long as I breathe.

That's not to say that I have not been blindsided or that my faith has not been tested.

One of the most heartbreaking, knee-buckling times of my life happened several years ago. Yet, as I sit here writing, it feels like yesterday. I thought I had met Mr. Right. He was charming, handsome, and successful. His family was fabulous, and he had a gorgeous three-year-old daughter. I fell in love with them all – hook, line and sinker. They loved me too, and we had five years of Christmas dinners, Easters, Thanksgivings, and birthdays. With my own family 900 miles away, I settled into what seemed like a dream. I felt I finally was going to have my 'whole' happiness.

We had a gorgeous house on the water, great jobs, a loving family, and I had a stepdaughter I loved as my own. Of course, there was an occasional speed bump along the way, but I loved my extended family so much that I ignored that little voice. You know the one. The one that nudges you and says, *Get a prenup* (Kanya was right on this one), or that something is not right.

I chose to ignore the signs. No matter how bright the flashing red bulbs were, I ignored my little voice. I had faith that it would all work out ok because I knew I deserved happiness.

We married. After we wed, he wanted to go on a guys' vacation with his friends. I trusted him, so it seemed ok to me at the time (I ignored my little voice again).

While he was gone, I received a call from a friend and employee that shook my world like an earthquake. This employee showed me emails, tapes and other items that proved my husband was self-admitted bisexual. There was no doubt that I had been deceived in one of the worst ways. The question in my husband's email read, 'So how long have you been gay?' My husband responded, 'I am bi, not gay. It increases my chances on a Saturday night by 50%.' I was married to someone I did not know and emotionally invested in his entire family.

Suddenly I was faced with complete devastation, humiliation, degradation, and worst of all, loss. Just to be clear, I don't care what your sexual preference is as long as you're not rocking my boat. Well, my boat was rocked like the Titanic.

I fell down the rabbit hole and hit the bottom, hard. I knew where this would lead and I wanted to un-ring this bell. I wanted my normal life back. Little did I know that the worst was yet to come.

I stayed silent for the next six months. I had to prepare for the death of the life I loved, the death of my marriage, and the death of my relationship with my stepdaughter. Anxiety and hate began to set in. How could he bring me into this?

Holding all this in was very debilitating and led to a severe anxiety attack. I knew it was over when my husband saw how anxious and stressed I was and did not show an ounce of concern. The coldness that came from him made Siberia look like the tropics.

I then threw a pity party for one. For three days, I lay in bed sobbing. I begged God to take me away from this heartache. I hoped and prayed that I wouldn't wake up because I couldn't face it all alone. On the third day, I screamed, "I am so alone! Why am I so alone? I don't want to be alone anymore!" I was done. Suddenly, my tears dried, my head cleared, and I heard my little voice. 'You are not alone. You have never been alone.' I felt those words deep in my core. I sat up in bed like a marionette snapping to attention at its puppeteers bidding. "What are you doing?" I said. "Get up and get on." I did just that. I got up, determined and clear of what I had to do. I ripped off the Band-Aid in one quick pull. I got an attorney, filed for divorce and a restraining order, changed the locks, and never looked back.

I made every single choice that led me to this exact spot. There was no one to blame. I knew that to get through this, I would need to pull every ounce of strength from my soul. The words 'you have never been alone' resonated inside my head and my heart. So I prayed, every day, all day. I would look to the sky, take a deep breath, and pray. For some, counseling is the answer, for others, it is the clergy. For me, it was God.

Don't throw a pity party – they're sad and lonely. The key is to picture your life the way you want it to be and then start living it as if it was that way. Be thankful for each moment, the good, the bad, and let's not forget – the ugly. If you believe your life is miserable, then it will be miserable. Conversely, if you believe your life is wonderful, you will also be right. It was my choice, and it is your choice. It's just like Neo from *The Matrix*; he had the choice between the red pill and the blue pill. Surround yourself with people who are happy and positive, even if that means you'll only have yourself for company! Smile even when you don't feel like it. It is contagious, and even you will catch it.

In the end (and there was one), I left that path behind and made a new one. One that is filled with wonderful experiences. The bottom line is that I made the choices that led to my path. No one held a gun to my head. I didn't listen to the little voice that has always been my guide. I now have its volume set to HIGH!

If we can accept that no one is to blame for the choices we make, maybe we can grow and heal without harboring hatred towards those who have wronged us. We were, and are, all participants. If you choose a path and it doesn't work out, or you don't like it, change your path. Complaining about your path and staying on it is acceptance. Our lives are not as the crow flies. We have some fun zigzags to experience, if we are lucky.

Smile and have faith. It's not just believing – it's knowing.

Rich Braconi

Rich Braconi is a self-taught spiritual life mentor, spirit medium and medical intuitive. Rich has discovered a process that allows him to remain spiritually centered and receive knowledge that only our spirit can interpret.

Raised Catholic, Rich spent twenty-seven years as an undercover narcotics detective, criminal investigations detective and member of the emergency response team.

Experiencing deep unhappiness in his mid-forties, Rich sought the truth about a co-existence with higher wisdom. Through an evidentiary effort, Rich unveiled an inner communication that allows him to receive knowledge from all sources of spiritual energy. Through word of mouth - Rich's spiritual workshops, spirit mediumship galleries, and spiritual mentorship classes have become a proven source of healing, insight, and awareness for thousands of people.

Find Rich online:

Website: www.ExpandingthePresence.com
Facebook:https://www.facebook.com/ExpandingthePresence/

Chapter 6

Living Spiritually Centered

By Rich Braconi

I was in my early forties when I was faced with divorce, enormous debt, separation from my daughter, depression and feeling alone, all while maintaining a stressful job of being an undercover narcotics detective. This part of my life was not something I ever planned for or would have wished for myself. Somehow, I unwisely managed to make choices that produced this unwanted situation. My biggest question was how did I manage to prevent myself from experiencing the loving existence that I had been seeking all my life? From my early childhood, I was raised a Catholic and was taught to place my faith in a universal God of great love. Yet, no matter how many times I prayed for God's helping hand to personally intervene and guide me in life; it just never came. This lack of help in my life caused me to lose my faith and feel abandoned.

Even though I reached a point in my life where I was barely surviving, I wasn't ready to give up on myself. I decided to challenge the so-called wisdom that was passed on to me by my religion, my parents, my education, my friends, and society. What if the majority of information I was taught by those sources was not the truth, and I was foolishly using this knowledge over and over again to find personal happiness, internal peace, contentment, and love. I was hoping that by not settling for just any life and empowering myself to seek a more profound understanding of it all that my effort would infuse some kind of positive change into my personal struggle. Realistically, I didn't have a clue how to begin. Do I turn to another religion, read spiritual books, consult a guru or just pray harder and more often? While contemplating my choices, I began to focus on what God is to me, if God really existed.

To me, for the moment, God was universal love, but what exactly is universal love and could its power change my life for the better? I sincerely believe that everyone wishes for loving relationships; to make choices that produce loving outcomes and to speak words that resonate a loving meaning, but where could I find the elusive understanding to make this all possible?

Even though love is something that people may strongly desire in their life, I cannot recall one single lengthy discussion where my family or my religion enlightened me with a working education about this mystical power. Arguably, love is the most equal opportunity force capable of enriching anyone's life. Yet, it is probably the most uncommon topic openly discussed within our families, our education, and our society. I have heard many people explain how love is light, love is unity and love is eternal. However, I desperately needed a real-world explanation about this universal force that I could use to transform my life.

Some of my questions were, where does love actually come from? How does a person get more of it? What prevents me from always acting and speaking in a loving way? Is universal love a divine communication that provides everyone with an equal ability to shift their own life in a more helpful direction?

I had so many questions that needed answers, but the one I needed an answer for the most was how could I demonstrate more love for me? Not knowing why I was doing it, I placed myself in a state of peace to ask myself this same simple question again. This resulted in an immediate sense that I needed to change what I focused my personal attention on. Somehow, I instinctively knew that shifting and focusing more of my personal attention to me first rather than giving it to others was the first step.

Then I was inspired by a sudden thought. Where did this inner knowledge I just received to shift my personal attention away from others and more towards myself originate from? I had no prior memory of reading this in a book or hearing someone suggest it to me. I then became very aware of how quickly this inner guidance came to me, much faster than my normal thinking process.

This inner guidance didn't suggest other options, like my thinking normally would, it communicated its statement as if this was the truth. It was up to me to have faith in it. It was as if I instantly knew the answer I asked to receive. To see if I could encourage another similar response, I again placed myself in a state of peace and truthfully asked myself, *Why do I need to focus more of my personal attention on myself rather than others?* Again, I was quickly filled with an inner sense that in order to understand how to be loving towards others I had to demonstrate love towards myself first. This made total sense to me. If I didn't demonstrate the knowledge and ability to maintain a loving life for myself, how else could I attain credible wisdom to be helpful to others?

A few moments later, while still in a state of peace, I strongly sensed that I was struggling for so long because I had been placing all my faith in the wrong source of guidance. I then began to examine the phrase, 'How do I help myself'. Who am I actually referring to when I say the word 'I' in that sentence? Am 'I' a physical body or am 'I' a physical brain or am 'I' a spiritual being? I knew this inner guidance that originally told me to change what I focus my personal attention on did not come from mental thinking. It was like how a real friend would make you feel when offering sincere insight that had a spiritual purpose. It was a guidance that inspired me with knowledge, while still giving me the freedom to choose to accept it or not. I also sensed that this guidance was the absolute truth and as it was communicated to me in a way that I would consider loving. Exploring an even deeper understanding of this experience helped me to realize that by speaking words in an inspirational way that doesn't interfere with another person's freedom I would be communicating in a more loving way.

I spent the next couple of weeks contemplating these experiences while searching for the right words to effectively explain this inner voice. My contemplation concluded with an explanation that permanently changed my perspective for the better. I now see myself as a spiritual being, not a physical body or brain. I have come to realize that every person has two different sources of personal guidance they can seek their wisdom from, and both compete for our personal faith.

One source of guidance comes from my mental thinking. However, on its own, my mental thinking is not capable of connecting to higher wisdom and does a very poor job discerning between what is real and what is not real. The second source of guidance I can follow comes from a divine source of higher wisdom, which can only be received through my spirit. This source feeds my spirit with universal truth that provides me with an education about a way of existence that is solely based on the communication of unconditional love. I also learned that whichever source of guidance I place my personal faith in would cause it to grow and expand. That means, for over forty years of my life, I mistakenly used my mental thinking as my means to attain spiritual peace, happiness, abundance, and love. Something my mental thinking was not created to do on its own.

The empowerment I gave to my mental thinking helped it to grow into a very dominant force. At the same time, my lack of faith in my spirit caused it to become very weak. There are three different strengths I can call upon to use for different purposes. First, I can call upon my body's physical strength. Secondly, there is my brain's mental strength. Thirdly, and most importantly, there is the strength of my spirit, which is my spiritual will. I also learned that whenever I quietened my thinking brain, a natural state of spiritual peace is experienced. I learned that it is my spirit that has the strength to quieten my mental thinking. However, if my spirit is weak, it will eventually lose this battle. This explains why, at first, I could only quiet my thinking for a very short period of time before it began again.

However, I still wasn't quite sure how to explain what love really is. So, again, I returned to a place of peace to ask myself questions about the power of love that I still needed answers for.

Over a four-week period, I made sure to keep detailed notes of any knowledge I received through my spirit. I figured if it was true that my spirit was receiving higher wisdom, then keeping detailed notes was demonstrating a level of respect and faith that it deserved. I was going all-in by demonstrating blind faith in the validity and credibility of my inner guidance until proven otherwise. At the end of the four weeks, I had over thirty pages of information that I can truthfully say didn't come from me.

Through my effort to seek a more expanded understanding of love, I was inspired by the following knowledge.

Pure and simple, love is a communication that is always spiritually helpful. It is a divine guidance that has the same universal effect on all people. If our words or actions are accomplished in a truly loving way, it will always result in an overall feeling of being personally helped. Being aided in a spiritual way means feeling supported, nurtured, understood, spoken to truthfully, and wisely guided. The communication of love is also the energy we spiritually sense that allows us to recognize the difference between people, places, opportunities and experiences that will benefit our life. We can learn valuable life lessons without suffering if we demonstrate the courage and faith to follow our inner guidance and wisdom unconditionally. Wisdom is the knowledge that profoundly explains how every aspect of our life is influenced by the communication of unconditional love or lack thereof. Wisdom is knowledge, but not all knowledge is wisdom.

Wisdom and love are two different things. Even though I speak wise words, I can still communicate those words in an unhelpful and unloving way. I can also communicate my words in a loving way without speaking wisdom. To give my words the greatest opportunity to be heard by others, I must demonstrate the ability to speak wise words in an unconditionally loving way. Otherwise, my words and actions will not produce a positive outcome. To communicate in an unconditionally loving way our words and actions have to be inspirational. Inspiration is the ability to communicate our words and actions without intruding on the free will of other people. Love is different from unconditional love. Love is being spiritually helpful, but still mentally wanting something in return for that help. Unconditional love is being spiritually helpful without mentally wanting something in return for our help. Our mental thinking is our biggest resistance and our greatest adversary towards enjoying a more spiritually centered and enlightening existence.

Over the next six months, I took this knowledge and incorporated into a daily way of life for myself. Being spiritual meant that I had to make a sincere willful effort to be the wisdom I said I had in order to give it an opportunity to change me truthfully. I found the more I placed my faith in the communication of my spirit (my inner voice), the easier it became to recognize it, the more often it occurred, and the more influential its growing strength had over me. Eventually, my spirit shifted to the forefront of my life, and it regained its original position as the more dominant role and influence.

For many years, my parents, society, and my schooling taught me to use my thinking as a means to receive anything I wanted a truthful answer for. However, using this method to seek a higher understanding of my life and myself often caused me to experience mental confusion, stress, anxiety, fears, and very often a sense of abandonment. Now, I was experiencing the opposite. Slowly but surely, all these mental side effects were replaced with internal peace, a sense of unity, a life of simple yet great accomplishment, and personal happiness. I now made choices that consistently resulted in loving outcomes.

Over the next couple of years, I continued to push the limits of maintaining a spiritually centered existence while improving the divine communication within my spirit. As a result, I have enjoyed a transformation of self, which has directly lead to many personal miracles and loving experiences that go beyond anything I originally was told I was capable of, including being inspired with a remedy to cure a man of stage 4 pancreatic cancer.

My life is now thriving in a direction that has no limitations. I am a retired police detective who has a flourishing and expanding business as an advanced spirit medium, spiritual life mentor, and medical intuitive. Through this transformation of self, wisdom and a greater ability to express myself in a more loving way, my relationship with my ex-wife improved greatly. I am now happily remarried to the woman I was once divorced from and consider her my very best friend. Everyday experiences are simple for me to understand; I am no longer in debt, and I enjoy the close relationship I always hoped for with my only daughter.

The most important life lesson I learned from all of this is that a spiritual co-existence and co-partnership has always existed between my spirit and a higher wisdom. I was unwisely taught at an early age to mentally break this contract and abandon this spiritual bond. By seeking the truth for myself, I learned how to surrender sole ownership of my life and re-establish my co-existence with God. Like I stated before, for many years I prayed for God's help, but I never believed that I received it. However, this is not the truth. My prayers were always being answered, but no one taught me that those answers could only be interpreted by my spirit. During our physical lifetime, every person will receive many opportunities to summon their own personal courage to support and choose what they spiritually sense a natural love for and what they spiritually sense is the truth. Unfortunately, not everyone will choose to live their life, courageously. Be courageous in yours!

Rala Brubaker

Rala is the founder of Live and Let Live and the creator of Joyful Adventures in Life Retreats and Coaching. Rala is a mother of three, an adventurous traveler, a planner, a little bit of a wild child and a social introvert! She believes everyone should live their lives fully, while allowing room for others to live the life intended for them. Through joyful adventures in life, she is currently in the process of creating her next big 'JoyVenture' in September of 2018 that will include pre and post group work with a joyful adventure in the middle. In addition, Rala has recently participated in a TEDX style speech and looks forward to sharing amazing conversations to encourage better dialog for everyone.

Find Rala online:

Website: www.justownyou.com
Facebook: www.facebook.com/ralajoy
Twitter: www.twitter.com/ralabrubaker

Chapter 7

How I Created My Joyful Adventure in Life

By Rala Brubaker

Where do I start? My childhood? My teen years where I used sex to feel loved? Perhaps from the beginning, when I realized that I was *just* surviving.

As I pounded the pavement again looking for a better day gig, I found myself thinking, *If I can just find a waitressing job in a cool club, THEN I will be happy.* It was the first time I became aware that I was happy to accept the crumbs. I wasn't looking to get ahead, to have more, and to do better. I truly felt I was only entitled to get by.

I had spent my entire life 'getting by' or merely surviving. My parents were young and poor. They both attempted to go to school to better themselves, but one of them had to drop out because I came along. They could manage with one kid, but another was just too much to juggle. My mother was excelling in her studies to be an office administrator, but my father was in the police academy. At that time, 1970's, his career held more weight.

Therefore, my mother quit her straight-A academic career so that my dad could finish his training.

Unfortunately, she never went back, so we were left in a never-ending cycle of poverty. My younger sister was born in a desperate attempt to keep a failing marriage together, which of course did not work. By the age of four, my parents were no longer able to maintain the façade and began the process of splitting up. I don't really remember my dad being around at all. When they were together, he worked the night shift, and we were always gone throughout the day so he could sleep. We were a family in passing.

Due to her lack of education, my mother struggled to put food on the table and unconsciously began to teach us that there wasn't enough in the world. We would need to work hard and have low expectations of life. If we did 'it' right we might get to marry above our current condition, but that was really the only hope. We were taught to be pretty, be quiet, and to make our men feel good. THEN we would be happy.

We moved often, every six months or so. I had a love-hate relationship with this lifestyle. I adored the freedom of knowing that if I hated our new home, we would move soon. I innately understood that I couldn't invest too heavily in others because they would soon be gone from my life. I had my sisters, and for a while, this was enough. We plodded along in life, learning how and when to be quiet in order to have our needs met, daydreaming about the ultimate rescue by the "knight on a white horse, whisking me off to a life of luxury and happiness".

I adapted, improvised, manipulated, and survived. As I became a teen, I began to recognize a distinct feeling of alienation from my dad. Now in all fairness to him, I was only getting one side of the story. My mother spent years struggling through jobs, repeated moves due to a lack of money and what I suspect was extreme self-doubt and loneliness. I know today that my parents did the best they could with the skills they had, and for me, that meant merely getting through life.

As a young adult, I set myself up to travel to Japan and live there for several months. Upon my return, I felt so emboldened that I loaded up my car with everything I owned, grabbed my last $200 bucks out of the bank (knowing I had a $200 car note due in three weeks), and headed for the 'promised land' of Los Angeles. I knew exactly two people in L.A. – one wasn't in town. The other was a male casting director that wanted me to sleep with him. I landed on his doorstep two days later and began to maneuver, manipulate and create my way into a job and a place to live. I knew I could keep him at bay for a few days. I was beginning to feel that I had some power and control over my life. I quickly met a family that lived in his building. They had two little girls they needed help with, so I became their temporary nanny. Now I had food and a place to stay without being chased around the couch. Within a week, I picked up a night and weekend job as a waitress, and I was on my way.

It was my willingness to take risks like going to Japan to model and moving to L.A. with nothing but a car that gave me the inkling that there was something more than surviving. For the first time in my life, I began to question what would fulfill me in life.

I started to study to be an actress. I used my portfolio from Japan to get some low-end modeling gigs, and I became more empowered. I loved feeling strong. It was at this point that I was introduced to a guy that opened my eyes to a possibility I had never known. Glenn was always on the top of the world, nothing ever seemed to get him down, and I wanted what he had. He slipped out of my life as quickly as he had entered it. I spent the next fifteen years referencing how he lived. I wanted to feel as free as he seemed – not a care in the world, everything always worked out for him in the best possible way.

I wanted his confidence, I wanted to know what I liked and what I didn't and be able to own that, but I didn't know how. So I did the work...I did everyone's work. I studied Wayne Dyer, Tony Robbins, Louise Haye, and Marianne Williamson. I read all the spiritual literature and fiction I could find...and I was miserable. I felt sad and lonely. I was still using sex to feel loved and safe even though I felt neither.

I made a choice to work at being an actress rather than messing around. I saw what it really took to succeed and did that. For the first time as an adult, I worked in the same way I had trained to become a competitive gymnast as a teen. I was terrified and exhilarated. I put 90% of my energy in my teen years into gymnastics so I would have somewhere to fit in and have ready-made friends every time we moved. In the end, I didn't get a worthwhile scholarship, and I definitely did not fulfill my Olympic dreams. What was going to happen if I put all my hard work into acting and it never panned out? What would that mean about me? That turned out to be the most important question I ever asked myself.

About four years later, after ten years in Los Angeles, I threw in the towel having achieved nothing as an actress. I walked away because I was bored. I was tired of just getting by and merely surviving. I wanted to live, be full of life, and feel amazing.

Incredibly, two months after I walked away, all my hard work began to pay off. I received numerous calls to audition for pilots and movies back in Los Angeles, but I didn't have the money to go to any of them. I did something I had never done before, I thought about my options…I could be upset that I was missing them or I could be appreciative that my skills as an actress were acknowledged. For the second time in my life, I chose to thrive.

I spent a short time in NYC. It didn't take long for me to know that I didn't want to live there. I found a way to move out and relocated to Colorado as I had met yet another man. Once again, I put my eggs in his basket. I did this out of fear of not being able to take care of myself. I mean, if he loved me enough to get me to Colorado then I *must* be worthy, right? In hindsight, this was one of my greatest defining moments on my journey to thriving.

I married this man, took on his ten-year-old son as my own, and had two more kids with him, only to end up miserably unhappy yet again. I began to wake night after night in a panic, wanting to run away and abandon it all. This was my wakeup call. Once again, I found myself surviving, just getting by. I was living a life that had more niceties: a fancy house, gorgeous kids, and great cars. It just wasn't fulfilling for me. I was thirty-two years old and back to square one.

I repeatedly attempted to 'fix' the situation. In the end, I realized that this was a much bigger process than I gave it credit for. I began to dive deeper and look for new types of teachers. I wanted to do more than just read the books. I knew I was going to have to make a huge leap, and I was scared.

I began to see that I was responsible for my surviving or thriving. The only place I could make a change was within me. I began to transition to thriving when I understood that I was the common denominator. I embraced the idea that the only person I could control was myself. If I didn't like my life, I had to be the one to grow and change it.

"Your life is your design. If you don't like the design...YOU have to be the one to change it!"

- Rala Joy Brubaker

This became my mantra. I have spent the last seven years getting conscious and intentional about my life. In order to do that, you must first be honest with yourself. We must first do the work to know, admit to, and finally embrace who we are before we can begin to share that with the world at large in a constructive way. I had spent my entire life getting by – surviving. I hid my hopes, dreams, and beliefs. I didn't want to dump my responsibility on others as I had seen so many women do while they attempted to 'be' who they are. I wanted to live and let live.

I was thirty-nine and living a life I had chosen, designed and created. Yet I was still merely surviving. There was no thrive, and there was no happiness. I didn't enjoy my kids. I loved and adored them, but I didn't know how to be joyful with them.

As I awoke at 3 am again one morning to the same old recurring nightmare, I chose to do something different. I got up and put my thoughts down on paper. I was honest with myself and owned up to things I knew I had been lying about. I began to see a clearer image of the life I wanted by asking myself, *What does my joyful adventure in life look like? What fills me with joy?* I still do this on a weekly basis. I assumed responsibility for creating my dream life, one that is worth living. I accepted that this is all a process that grows and recedes on a day-to-day basis. I have amazing days, and I have days where would like to stay in bed. I honor those moments as they are the ones that propel me forward in my next steps to my best version of ME. I accepted that to thrive doesn't always mean to be at the top of the world. To thrive means I am always in a state of growth, with a willingness to go forward honestly each moment as ME. A willingness to live in a new vision of each activity, moment, and day. When I screw up or find myself being judgmental, I thrive by owning it and examining why I feel this way. When I am exhausted to the point of not being able to handle others, I thrive by committing to self-care.

Thriving is an attitude, a commitment, a willingness to be honest. Be human, and give yourself a do-over when you need to. A belief that I share with Maya Angelou is, 'When we know better, we do better.' I desire to be the best version of me that I can be today, and I look forward to what that version looks like tomorrow.

I leave you with this from the movie Eat, Pray, Love, 'When we are learning something new we must be polite with ourselves.'

Be polite with yourself. Embrace your humanity and know that learning takes time. The goal is not the outcome; it is how you go about creating your joyful adventure along the way.

Darlene Fandrey

Darlene believes her purpose is to be an encourager to the average person, there are so many of us. She achieved her BA certificate at the age of sixty-nine.

After twenty plus years working in the healthcare field, at seventy-four Darlene is most grateful for the ability to work full-time, live on her own, hop in the car and go places.

Darlene has survived many situations so hopes to light a path to peace in a much shorter time. She is living proof life can be restored one verse at a time.

Find Darlene online:

Email: restoringthesoul@twc.com

Chapter 8

From Shifting Sand to Solid Rock

By Darlene Fandrey

I had made it through many traumatic situations, but this was really something else! Cancer!

In between treatments, when you have no idea if you will make it, and you have a lot of time to reflect. You search for reasons to endure this awful weakness, and I believe my purpose was to survive and encourage others that they could too.

Shortly after my surgery, my daughter's job transferred her a hundred miles away. Most weekends, she drove back and forth from Columbus to Cincinnati to check on me. I hated being such a burden, even though she did not make me feel that way.

When they moved to Columbus, my daughter started looking for a place to take my granddaughter Easter egg hunting. While driving through town, she saw a sign for an event. On Easter Sunday, they went to check out World Harvest Church and fell in love with it. God goes all out to draw us in if we just look for the signs!

They invited me to come and join them. I wasn't much for church going at the time. Old wounds from churchy type people hadn't healed. I'd been brought up to think there was only one religion that counted, and if you weren't a part of that, you were doomed. I'd been grounded for a whole month after attending another denomination's service, so it never crossed my mind to go anywhere else. As far as I could tell, God had favorites, and I wasn't one of them.

I've found since then that there are many in that boat; people that were excommunicated from their church and believe that God has abandoned them. I met a lady whose parents were both ministers and when she went away to college and started wearing lipstick, they ran her out of the church, calling her a harlot!

When religious folk wonder why their churches are empty, the bars are full, and the drug dealers are thriving, they might want to check out their welcoming committee. Somehow, they have missed the part where Jesus said, "repent". That was Jesus' first message when He started His ministry.

It was my grandkids that had given me a purpose and inspired me to keep going when I was at the end of my rope. So on a lovely spring day in 2012, I made the trip to Columbus.

On the way to church, my little great-granddaughter could hardly wait to get to children's church! That was exciting! When I was a child, they didn't have anything like that, and I remember being pinched and poked in an effort to make me stop squirming in my seat. Shamefully, I remember doing the same to my own kids trying to keep them respectful of being in church.

We have to forgive those who came before us, especially if they are not here to question them. Somehow, people tend to try to motivate us by pointing out our flaws or weak areas. For instance, you might get three As on your report card, but one C is where the focus is. If only you had studied harder, you could have gotten all As. I am guilty of this myself and wish I could go back and change it.

I found a quote some time ago that has helped me immensely. I don't know the author.

'I forgive you for not being who I wanted you to be. I forgive you and set us both free.'

Many of the issues we have in this life are because we are expecting, wanting, and wishing for someone to be something that they are not. My whole life I was addicted to being liked. When we allow someone else to set our value or rely on them to make us happy, we wind up feeling like we've been in the spin cycle of the washing machine too long.

You may believe that God has no idea of who you are, or that He is so mad at you that there is no hope. He knows every detail of your heart, and He is very patient. He will never force Himself on you, and He has a sense of humor too! Once upon a time I would have thought what came next was just a coincidence.

As we were being seated, I noticed a young girl walking down the aisle with a tiny baby on her shoulder. Just then, Pastor Parsley came onto the platform and saw her with her head down. He said, "Oh no! Lift your head. All of that is in the past."

Next, he walked over to his daughter and took a ring from her finger and placed it on that young woman! I'd never seen or heard anything like that in my life. Tears started flowing uncontrollably as a memory almost fifty years prior came back! I couldn't believe my eyes or ears! I couldn't help but wonder what my life might have been like if something like that happened to me.

I later found out our church supports the Women's Clinic of Columbus where they not only save babies from being aborted but give the mothers parenting classes, teach them about nutrition, get them medical attention and so much more. That's only one of fourteen ministries the World Harvest Church supports. It's an amazing place!

I really wasn't so sure I was going to survive that bout with cancer, so I decided to move to Columbus so my daughter could stop running back and forth. I went willingly to the next service. That time Pastor said, "If I can get you to change who you are listening to, you can change your life." They passed out plans to read the Bible in a year. I took one. (I had actually purchased a Bible a few years before and started at the beginning but I got stuck. My tongue became tied trying to pronounce the names. I later learned that God put all those names in to let us know how important each and every one of us is.) One verse at a time, life started flowing through me again.

Next, I took the thirty-day challenge from the Christian Radio station. I switched from the crying in my beer country to contemporary Christian, turning the dial on the car and house radio. When you have nothing to lose and everything to gain, you might as well try it, right?

Another Sunday, Pastor said, "I don't know how you will fix this, Lord, only that you will." He attributed it to Habakkuk 3:1-19. I had no idea who the heck Habakkuk was, but I liked the message and wrote it on a slip of paper to research.

I had a lot of things that needed fixing at the time. I needed a hip replacement, but I wanted to have hope I was going to survive cancer before I spent any more money that I didn't have. However, now that my grandson was getting married it suddenly became more important to get that hip fixed. I wanted to be able to dance at his wedding!

God works in strange ways. When I called to make the appointment, the scheduler only had them way in the future, and there would not be enough time to heal before the wedding. The other line rang, and she put me on hold. When she came back, she said she just had a cancellation and if I wanted to come in on Tuesday, she could put me on the schedule. This was a Friday! You see how He works out little details for us. I had my surgery and there was plenty of time to recuperate! I got to dance at my grandson's wedding! And what a time that was.

By now, I'd owed a lot of money, and it became clear that I would need a full-time job if I didn't want to leave a pile of debt as my legacy.

I'd been applying unsuccessfully for a while and I nearly lost hope. Who would want to hire an old lady (almost seventy-two), when young whippersnappers couldn't get a job?

Still, I'd been a tither and giver out of my small pension and was standing on God's promise in Philippians 4:19, that my He would meet all my needs. I was actually reading the book of Habakkuk when I got the call that I'd been hired for a full-time position a very short distance from home. That was two months before my seventy-second birthday. I'm still there as I type this chapter.

I believe that God has given me the opportunity to share my story to encourage others that He is still turning water into wine, giving sight to the blind and healing the sick. He doesn't play favorites.

He truly has made us all wealthy. We would realize that if we just stopped and counted our blessings. If you are reading this, you are breathing, using your sight and holding onto a book, which means you have some mobility and a working brain. If you are enjoying a cup of coffee or some other refreshment, you have the gifts of taste and smell. Who would take a million dollars for any of those gifts?

Here I am, a person with only a high school education, getting to write a chapter in a book with people that have all sorts of degrees after their name. It took me sixty-nine years to get my BA certificate. The BA stands for born again, and that has made all the difference. You can do it much quicker!

My greatest regret is that I did not instill faith in God in my family as they were growing up. However, we cannot give what we do not have. We cannot teach what we do not know, and we cannot help when we don't understand. But we can learn. Therefore anything we hope to pass on to our children, we must first learn ourselves.

I was in total shock to find out one of my daughters always felt unimportant when I thought she had the world by the tail! We think they know we love them by providing every electronic gadget known to man. Yet, there are so many signs that our children are not feeling valued, even though our credit card debt is staggering and the suicide rate keeps climbing. Why would this be happening if our youth felt they had value?

We're doing something wrong. We have taken God out of the schoolroom and replaced Him with people teaching safe sex, and if that doesn't work, there is always abortion as a method of birth control. Somehow, we've gone from throwing everyone out to believing anything is ok.

The world is sorely in need of God. Our nation was founded on Christian principles. By just following the Ten Commandments, we could eliminate lies, stealing, killing, and jealousy.

God, however, is a gentleman and will not force Himself on us. He will let us spin around until we're dizzy or until we cry out for mercy. When we do, that's how we move from shifting sand to solid rock. I am living proof that you can restore your soul, one verse at a time.

I'm sure, had I been soaking in the word of God when trauma occurred, it would not have overcome me. Anyone that thinks they can use liquid courage to make things more bearable is heading toward a very slippery slope that will take them places they don't want to go.

Being a Christian doesn't mean you will never have trouble, it just means there is something inside of you that says get back up and try again! God will never require anything of you that would cause you to feel ashamed.

I'd like to challenge anyone who is feeling stressed to the max to build a stress buster kit: a Bible, reading plan, notebook to write stuff you may want to tear up, a journal for writing things you want to keep, and a pen. Pour positives into your life. Stop listening to music that takes you back to broken relationships and causes you to relive those sad times. Music is very powerful! We can go years without hearing a song and remember all the lyrics. The right words and music can also lift your spirits. In order to change your life, you have to do something different if you're hoping for different results. It is so simple. The challenge may not be easy, but it is worth the effort.

Surround yourself with people that encourage you. You won't believe the difference it will make!

I Am

I am a child of God,

No one else has permission to set my value.

I am strong because the joy of the Lord is my strength.

I am compassionate because I have felt the pain of condemnation.

I am trusting in God,

Even when I feel like I've been in the spin cycle

of the washing machine too long!

I need only to look at the butterfly,

To know that His plans for me

Are so much better than anything I could think of on my own.

I no longer accept other's opinion as truth

just because they are in a position of power.

When I start feeling overwhelmed,

I go off to a quiet place and pray

Until I remember whose I am.

Now the legacy I hope to leave behind for my children, grandchildren, and future generations is that they are children of God – always loved and valued. It doesn't matter if your parents come home from work tired and grumpy, or if the neighborhood bully has attacked you, or that a boss or co-worker has tried to tear you down.

As a child of God, be confident and secure that you are loved and cherished. Should you want that for your family and don't know where to start, try logging on to www.whc.life. While all our services are awesome, the one on December 17, 2017, was so powerful and was taught by the children.

Should you accept my invitation, you will be blessed.

"You may choose to look the other way, but you can never say again that you did not know."

\- William Wilberforce

Jennifer Fraser

Jennifer is an award-winning teacher, researcher and author. She has been featured in the media many times. Jennifer advocates for the rights of students and individuals to learn in an abuse-free environment.

Since the publication of her third book, Jennifer has been giving interviews and across North America about the impact abuse and bullying have on our brains. She launched a summit to end bullying and abuse in sport, and developed a twelve-course certification to change attitudes towards bullying.

With a PhD in Comparative Literature from the University of Toronto, Jennifer's approach is research-based, but in her spare time, she enjoys writing thrillers.

Find Jennifer online:

Websites: https://www.pushboundconsulting.com/
           http://jennifer-fraser.com/
GoTime Learning Summit:
           https://gotimelearning.com/end-bully-stop-abuse-in-sports-summit/
Twitter: https://twitter.com/teachingbullies
Facebook: https://www.facebook.com/TeachingBullies/

Chapter 9

From Reader to Writer

By Jennifer Fraser

I've always loved to read. The first book I remember reading was *Are You My Mother?* It was about a duckling who'd somehow been separated from her family and was going around asking other creatures, and even a front-end loader if in fact, they were her mother. In grade five, I read all the volumes of *Anne of Green Gables* and *Little House on the Prairie*. Then in grade six, I re-read them. An aunt gave me a box full of Harlequin Romances that I devoured while traveling by train across Canada but realized around the seventieth one that it was actually the same story being told over and over again. While familiar and soothing, it got a bit boring.

In grade seven, my mother steered me off this brainless track by handing me *Pride and Prejudice* which I struggled through, lying on my stomach under the apple tree in our backyard in Vancouver. With that done, I was next given the Bröntes. I enjoyed *Wuthering Heights* much more than *Pride and Prejudice*, as the terrifying knock at the window and the violent, jealous feelings were much more relatable to my childish mind than the arch turns of phrase Austen used to contemplate marriage. *Jane Eyre* was my favorite though, as Jane's terrible temper, and perseverance through unspeakable cruelty, created a space for me to hear my own rage, and experience my own wounds, without fearing they would consume me.

At twenty, I was confined to a darkened room in Mykonos, due to an abruptly discovered sun allergy that covered my neck and arms in hives under the glaring Grecian sun. My solace was the dense prose of Joseph Conrad that described a dark heart that beat in humanity and made me wonder at our capacity for forgiveness or renewal.

My professors at college opened my mind up to Shakespeare and Dante. Kate Sirluck would never lecture us, she'd simply flip open up a play like *King Lear*, and say: "Act I, scene i, line 1." We'd open up our books, and she'd read: "I thought the king had more affected the Duke of Albany than Cornwall." She'd gaze up at us, blinking behind her glasses, and ask with the urgency of a detective at a crime scene: "What's going on?"

We'd begin to offer suggestions, which she would transform into rich psychological insights and remarkably articulated ideas that left me literally breathless. Sometimes I'd leave class with my heart beating so fast that I'd have to consciously calm down. I had never heard anyone speak the way she did or analyze characters as if they were living, breathing psychological conundrums we had to diagnose. One day she arrived to class late and told us her car had broken down. It gave me a jolt because I believed her more likely to arrive on campus seated on the back of a black swan.

My Dante prof, Marguerite Chiarenza, who always spoke as though she had a cigarette dangling from the corner of her mouth, with a slight southern accent, made the *Divine Comedy* a riveting experience of navigation, exploration, being lost and found in the spiritual landscape after death. The soul became, in her classroom, a place where one could peer in and question its darkness or be taken aback by its light.

I loved reading so much that after I completed a double BA, dragging it out an extra year to finish all the coursework, I figured an MA would buy me some more time in the library. After that, I settled happily in for five more years of reading while doing my PhD. I felt smug about the fact that everyone thought that I was working hard, when in reality, I was simply creating the necessary conditions to keep reading. I lost myself in Virginia Woolf and stumbled through James Joyce. I spent months reading Proust's *Remembrance of Things Past* and plowed through the different theories on what stories meant, why people read, the construction of 'other', the deconstruction of binaries and so on. There were feminist, economic, queer, racial, religious, philosophical, and linguistic lenses to look through. There were endless ways to think about, discuss, question and interpret books. Analyzing stories and writing about them was all that was needed for me read and read and read.

Next step was lecturing. I liked teaching because it meant I could not only talk about reading, but also learn a great deal from my students about their reading experience, which was fascinating and revealed to me new perspectives and layers to the stories I so cherished. I could write pages and pages about reading, and ultimately, university presses published my thoughts in books.

My days of reading fiction came to an abrupt halt one night when a mother called me in tears about her child who was being harmed. Her son had texted her saying, 'I can't take it anymore'. He reported that the boys were being called "f***ing embarrassments" and "f***ing retards" by their teachers, my colleagues who worked in the P.E. department.

I was shaken. I reported to the headmaster. I learned from a parent who was a lawyer that the headmaster had been informed a year before about 'child abuse' occurring at the hands of these teachers and he had not stopped it. I took testimonies from eight students at the headmaster's request. The students were being harmed within the very school that gave me my livelihood. I could not afford to lose my job. As I took notes, while students both girls and boys, told me disturbing details about how these teachers mistreated them, I began to feel afraid. A question was forming within me as the boys told about how one student in particular was a target for the teachers. This boy would be publicly shamed over and over.

The players would have to watch as the teacher yelled in this boy's face, questioning his value and his right to even play. When the boy would try and get away, the teacher would grab him and hold him in for more. The other teacher would watch. I finally asked myself the question: Who was this boy?

"Monty."

The name hit me like a blow to the gut. At that moment, those teachers, the headmaster and his administrators who served his agenda crossed a line. Everyone has within them an invisible line. For James Joyce, that line runs right down the center of the colonial system. For Dante, it delineates heaven and hell. For Virginia Woolf, it is a glass wall dividing male privilege from female rights. When I heard that name, reported by those boys, a line got crossed.

Monty is my son.

The school's chaplain, the headmaster's right-hand man, sent me an email saying that if I kept quiet, Monty would be protected, but the other kids would not have that same privilege. I know my son very well. He would never look the other way while other kids were being hurt. He would never lie to keep a false and harmful system in place that protected abusers and re-victimized students. I had always liked and admired the school chaplain, but the deal he wanted to make meant compromising my son's integrity and stepping back over the line into a school I now knew to be teaching corruption, instead of goodness. I had no choice.

***

I am much happier in a library with a book than I am speaking up, standing up, voicing my concerns, stating an ultimatum, but I could not work in a school where teachers were allowed to harm students. I knew enough after eight years in this private school that the headmaster, and administrators like the chaplain who served his agenda, would look the other way when abuse was reported by students. I knew they would sweep it under the carpet. I'd seen them do it before. I could clearly see my choice: stay as a reader of the story written by the school where I worked, or resign in protest, and leave as the writer of a story constructed on truth and a refusal to remain silent when children were being harmed. I handed in my resignation.

It was a painful choice on many levels. It's comfortable being a reader. It's like going to chapel where someone else has written the sermon. It's a play happening on stage where the script is written, and you must merely play your part. As long as you don't think, and say your lines on cue, you get to belong to the community. You get paid every two weeks. I wanted to stay as a reader more than anything. I retreated for one last time into my library.

There was *Are You My Mother?* It was about asking questions and finding the truth. *Anne of Green Gables* was about being an orphan and learning to create a family. *Little House on the Prairie* was about survival. *Jane Eyre* tore apart the education system exposing its hypocrisy and cruelty. Conrad led readers down the terrifying path of colonialism while Joyce used wild humor to destabilize it. Woolf opened up the minds and delved into the hearts of female characters so that women became three dimensional in her stories. I ran my hands along the spines of these books. The only way that Dante could find the courage and wisdom to spiral down into hell was because he was accompanied by Virgil, author of the *Aeneid*. The first academic study I wrote was about this mentoring relationship. I wrote about the rite of passage from being a reader of culture to a writer of culture. I left the safety of my library, remembering my first book.

I made my choice. I spoke with a voice that was constructed by these many authors. I had developed empathy with my cherished colleagues. I stepped away from the well-groomed path of my community and culture and set forth on the rocky path of writing a story the headmaster and his administrators did not want to acknowledge, let alone hear. I learned that asking questions made people uncomfortable. Deviating from the script, opened me up to attack, but I still refused to swerve from the writing path. When they couldn't reach me, they sought out my son with the hope that this would silence us.

They made the mistake of thinking that if they hurt him even more, he would not be able to stay true to his course. They didn't know that Monty had set as his goal when he was sixteen to "not let them break me". They didn't know that even as a teenager, he had a steely comportment that kept him immune to their threats and jibes.

When you stop being a reader and choose to be a writer, the blinders that once made you able to enjoy the chapel of your culture fall from your eyes, and you must witness the system's lie. When you find and trust your voice, writing what you know to be true, the chaplain with his false pillars reveals his true face.

Gazing into that monstrous visage, despite the suffering I endured in speaking up, I knew I had made the right choice.

When the Dalai Lama was asked how it was possible that he could act and speak compassionately about China, he replied that they had taken so much from him that he would not let them take his compassion. The headmaster caused my son and me intense pain, but I still feel sorry for him. I can't think of anything worse than being him.

When I stopped being a reader of culture and crossed the line into being a writer, I discovered that the community constructed by this private school would collapse. As this house of cards fluttered away, it revealed a bedrock foundation of people strong enough to push back against the weight of an ignorant and apathetic culture that condones bullying and abuse, all the while insisting they won't be tolerated. The school took a lot from me, but they could not crush the compassion and courage I found to speak up. And Montgomery has never looked back.

Literature (not just escapist fiction) does not give us information. It does not make us knowledgeable or offer us prestige. Reading the stories of great writers provides us with courage, challenges us to be authentic, and foregrounds individuality as a key component of community. Reading the stories of great writers opens up a well of empathy within us into which we can drop buckets during our struggles and crises. While the empathy makes it difficult or impossible to ignore the pain of others, and activates within us an ethical and compassionate response, it also enables us to feel the anguish of those who perpetrate or cover up abuses. What I learned in my shift from being a reader, or one who was surviving, to being a writer, and one who was thriving was the need in all of our lives to find the time for great literature.

Eileen Jason,
Ph.D., MBA, PMP, GC-C

Dr. Eileen Jason is an organizational psychologist and president/CEO of ARTA Consulting, LLC, a firm that provides consulting in leadership, employee motivation, and satisfaction for business and individuals. Dr. Jason is also an AAGC Certified Grief counselor. She is passionate about helping people interact with awareness – particularly in today's seismic shifting world! After experiencing the cataclysmic movement of her own tectonic plate, Dr. Jason decided to help people who are undergoing shifts of their own. She is the author of Factors Affecting Leadership Trust and currently hosts Corporate 911 – a talk show that addresses issues within the workplace.

Find Dr. Eileen online:

Website: http://artaconsulting.com/
LinkedIn: https://www.linkedin.com/in/eileenjason/
You Tube: https://www.youtube.com/channel/UCBCrWWmy
          CeWHfyyjzRjyNsg?view_as=subscriber

Chapter 10

Death Is Just a Stepping-Stone

By Eileen Jason

I am so grateful for the life I have chosen. If someone were to say those words to me as I was growing up (as a Catholic), I most certainly would have thought they were going straight to hell. Among other beliefs as a Catholic person, I was taught to believe that a single entity – a man – was sitting in heaven manipulating all that takes place on earth, including placing a person in a particular life situation and calling 'all of the shots' throughout their lifetime. That's what good, obedient Catholic children were taught. You were just supposed to accept your fate and go through life as best you could, while fearing the worst if you'd done something to displease the one single entity who could banish you for all eternity.

If you think about it, it's frightening. One wrong turn or incident of imperfect behavior and you could end up in a place where you certainly do not want to be for the rest of time. Even as a child raised in a Catholic household and attending Catholic schools, I did not feel the same connection to the Catholic religion as my parents – particularly my dad. I remember my father once telling me that if I did not attend mass every week, I would most definitely end up in hell. I thought it very odd that missing one mass could do that to me. Who were these priests that held so much power over me to tell me I would go to hell if I did not attend a weekly mass? I thought it was very odd that women were not allowed to be priests or have any power or authority in the church, and in fact, only men could 'absolve me of my sins'. It just never felt right to me.

As I look back on my life during those times, I realized that those feelings were my intuition, my true-self telling me that I had a whole lot to learn about what true spirituality was, and how future events in my life would shepherd me the most to the profound and powerful experiences.

When I was twenty-six, my mother passed away suddenly and unexpectedly from a massive heart attack, two days before Thanksgiving. I was at the local shopping mall that night. When I returned home, there was a note on the door to go to the hospital. By the time I arrived, my mother had already passed. In fact, I was to learn later that she passed away before the paramedics arrived at the house. I was able to see her one last time to say my goodbyes while she was lying on a hospital table. Thanksgiving that year, and for many years later, was never the same.

My mother was the life of the party. She had so many friends, and everyone who met her liked her immediately. My father, who was typically very stoic, broke down and cried on Thanksgiving Day. The picture of him sobbing is forever etched in my memory. I felt utterly helpless. There was absolutely nothing I could do to make him feel better. It was a scene I will never forget. I remember thinking that our lives were changed forever and would never be the same. The only semblance of comfort I felt was knowing that she was in heaven. I knew that because in spite of her not attending mass every week, she was the most compassionate person I knew. She taught me by her actions to treat everyone with respect and kindness. She could be in no other place.

As I look back on that particular experience, I recall feeling a deep sense of loneliness. I was the youngest of four children, and I was the only child that was not married or who had kids. It was an unspoken fact that I was to take care of my dad, because I had 'no life' as far as my siblings were concerned. Even many years later, I was still expected to take care of my dad because even though I did become involved with someone, I did not have children. Therefore, my life was not as important as my siblings' lives. I will always be grateful for the time I spent with my dad. I felt that we grew closer as he aged. It wasn't always easy; he was not a very emotional person, but I appreciated and loved him. I recall having many conversations with him about the Catholic religion, especially as I was moving away from its tentacles. He always said he was worried about me, particularly about where I would go after I died, but I never wavered in my belief that I would be fine. I told him that when we meet in the afterlife, he would surely agree that there was something else besides the Catholic religion.

Life went on after my mother passed, albeit at times things were extremely difficult. I did not realize how my mother's death affected me with regard to relationships. Looking back, I realize how much I feared having a serious relationship with someone because I was afraid they were going to leave me by dying. I went about my life for the next several years without dating anyone very seriously – at least not enough to spend the rest of my life with them.

Then I met him, Art, the man I was to spend the next seventeen years with. I was working at a company and managing a computer department at the time. I remember the day as if it were yesterday. I remember what I was wearing, and I remember what he was wearing. I remember feeling – or rather knowing – as we were being introduced that I recognized this man somehow. Not the feeling that we met before at another place or through mutual friends. There was a very distinct familiarity with him. I didn't know what it was, but it was certainly an energy that existed between us. Later, as we got to know each other, he said he felt the same.

He was very kind, handsome, and probably the smartest man I have ever – or will ever – meet. I felt that I could finally 'let go' and relax knowing that he would always be there for me (and I for him). It was a sense of relief knowing that we could share our life experiences and lean on each other when necessary. Family and friends noticed. They often commented that there was a deep connection between us and often wondered how two people could be so compatible. We traveled every year, often twice a year, to an island for warmth or skiing in the colder weather.

Life was good...until my father passed away in August of 2010. I was so grateful to have the family together for his eighty-second birthday a few months earlier. Although he was fully cognizant and still driving, he had recently had gallbladder surgery, and I knew something was not right. Again, my intuition was telling me this, but I did not recognize it at the time. I received the call late at night and had to go to the hospital to say my goodbyes. He had already passed by the time we arrived, but I was comforted by the fact that he was in a good place and very grateful for getting to know him and spending more time with him in my adult years.

Again, the feeling of knowing that he was in a good place, but not wholeheartedly believing in the heaven and hell scenario was what got me through his passing. I still think of him often and even talk to him on occasion. I know he – as well as my mother –

are still around me now in spirit (even though Dad might have disagreed with that sentiment while he was here on the earth plane).

While the death of a parent is difficult, it is inevitable. In the circle of life, it is intended to happen that way. I believed they were both in a good place and that I would see them again someday.

I had a great life with Art, and things were going well. Then it happened. The day that I will never forget. It was by far the darkest, loneliest, and most heart wrenching period of my life. It turns out also that it was the day I would become who I was meant to be. My spiritual journey would take me through the most interesting and awakening voyage that I could ever possibly imagine – all with Art by my side in spirit.

At first, it appeared to be food poisoning, but then turned into a horrific three and a half month roller coaster ride of tumultuous ups and downs; being hopeful one day to bone-crushing numbness the next. After being admitted, the hospital started running tests to see if they could determine the cause of his pain. They sedated him and gave him pain medication. I consider myself an optimistic person and the thought of him not recovering never entered my mind. Naturally, I believed the doctors would find the cause, fix it, and we would go on living happily ever after. I stayed with him the entire day, but since we lived alone with just the two of us, I had to attend to our dog. I went home late in the evening, did what I needed to do around the house, and fully expected to return in the morning to take him home.

However, the universe had other plans. His conditioned worsened within hours of being admitted. He was in such extreme pain the doctors medically induced a coma in the middle of the night. The hospital called to let me know what was happening and by the time I returned, he was fully induced.

For the next three and a half months, he was to remain in this medically induced coma, have several operations, and endure a hospital transfer. For me, this period was, to say the least, surreal. Through it all, I never gave up hope that he would survive and continued to speak with him and hold his hand every day and night, until the day the surgeon and his chief doctor said he would not be going home. I remember making the most difficult decision of my life to take him off life support. I was numb.

It was October 12, 2012. I stayed the entire night with him in the hospital. My birthday was October 11ᵗʰ. Since he spent the night of his birthday in the hospital in July, I felt it was the least I could do to spend mine with him in the hospital as well. He managed to live through the night; a selfless gesture I believe, so that I would not remember the tragedy happening on my birthday.

As I write this chapter five years later, I am crying. I've never spoken about what I endured or how utterly painful it was for me after his passing. I don't have the words to describe the complete and total sensation of loneliness, the dark hole I found myself in, the gut-wrenching sobbing that would put me to sleep on far too many occasions. I would tell people that the feeling was similar to losing my right arm; I would survive, but life would never be the same, and I would have to learn to adjust.

When people experience a death of someone who is so close to them, typically there is a support system to help them get through their grief. I didn't feel I had that support system. None of my siblings came to the hospital the day it happened. My oldest brother who had cancer was fearful that he might also die from going to the hospital. My sister was living in Florida so she could not be there to support me. My other brother started a new job and felt it was more important to stay on the job. Art's family completely disengaged and blamed me for what they perceived was my inability to 'take care' of him. When I returned to work, my co-workers didn't know what to say, so they barely said anything. My boss at the time was more concerned about the job at hand than showing any comfort and compassion. My neighbors were busy with their own lives.

I felt completely alone and desolate, as though someone punched me in the heart. There were many days where I did not have the strength to get out of bed in the morning, and looked forward to nighttime when I could return to dreamland and pass the time. I had no idea how to move forward. Of the many emotions I experienced, the greatest was the sorrow I felt at not having the chance to tell Art I loved him before the medically induced coma. The inability to have a conversation for those three and a half months was torture.

It was at this darkest time in my life that I decided I needed to know what happens in the afterlife. As I mentioned, you expect parents to pass, and at the time of my parents' passing, I felt that they were in a good place. However, when Art passed, it was too much for me to simply assume he was in a better place. I lost my soulmate and my best friend. I felt compelled to find meaning in his passing. This newfound desire for meaning propelled me. I managed to take tiny steps forward on my own, one day at a time.

It is no coincidence that I was guided to books, people, and experiences that would help me understand the journey that would change my entire belief system from the obedient Catholic girl to one with true belief that there *is* life after death. Death is just a stepping-stone to our experience and learning. We *do* choose our lives on this earth plane, specifically and intentionally for the challenges and learning experiences we are undertaking. We are not alone. It is truly exciting!

My oldest brother who had cancer passed away two years after Art. I was able to comfort my sister-in-law with the belief that he is still with us. Just as everyone else who has crossed over, there is more learning to do and much more to experience.

I resigned from my corporate profession not long after Art passed; that chapter of my life was over. It was the beginning of truly listening to my intuition and trusting it. I knew corporate life was no longer my path. I started my own consulting business after compelling myself to finish my Ph.D. in organizational psychology. I recently added grief counseling to my service offerings. I hope to help people understand that while death is tragic, it's not the end. Once I began truly believing in life after death, synchronous events started taking place, and there would be no more coincidences in my life. Everything is happening as planned and agreed upon (by the universe and me).

There is no doubt in my mind that Art is still with me – as well as my mother, father, brother, and all other loved ones who have crossed over. I see real, tangible signs from Art as well as him visiting me in my dreams. It may seem crazy to say that I feel closer to him now as I continue on my spiritual journey! I know now that I chose to experience this event and others in isolation. It is my journey that I needed to take by myself.

I have new and different friends, and people I call 'like-minded' that I surround myself with these days. My journey is continuing, and I learn something new every day. I look forward to the time when I meet again with Art and other loved ones, but I know I have much to do here to help people.

While it is true that everyone takes their own journeys and experiences life differently, my heartfelt suggestion for anyone who finds themselves going through a tremendous shift would be to talk to professional if you feel the need. Find time for yourself and spend time with family and friends if they support you. Do whatever you feel you need to do to get through a painful situation. Most of all, grieve in your own time, at your own pace, and never let anyone tell you that 'it's time' to move on and forget that person or those people you lost. You will move forward, but it will be at your own pace, and you will be grateful for the experience you shared with those special loved ones!

From surviving to thriving, I am grateful for the life I've chosen!

Shelley Jaye

Shelley Jaye is a wise woman of intrigue, strength, courage and enlightenment. A massage practitioner since 1989, she co-developed 'The Gift of Touch' massage experience, which was part of the Anatriptic Arts Exposition with Massage Magazine. She has assisted women through the birthing process, created an herbal apothecary for family and friends, home-birthed and holistically raised four creative, loving children.

Embodying an entrepreneurial spirit, and a strong singing voice, Shelley - a recipient of the Athena® Leadership Award - holds a BA in Education and Human Ecology from Vermont College and an MFA Creative Writing at Goddard College is in progress. She is the embodiment of divine feminine.

Find Shelley online:

Facebook: https://www.facebook.com/ShelleyJWriter/
Websites: https://wordpress.com/stats/day/sjteaches.
wordpress.com
https://www.timplistic.com/

Chapter 11

Find Your Spirit and Take a Stand

By Shelley Jaye

My journey is one of self-healing and learning to trust Spirit to lead me through the process of being a healer. There is no one specific moment that spontaneous healing occurred, it happened in stages as I learned to quiet my mind and listen to Spirit. Take a deep breath or two and read on, I will a share my story with you.

On a July night many years ago, I was sleeping in my bed in a quiet suburban townhouse community, my child snuggled by my side. I opened my eyes to find a gun pointed at my face by a masked person. Time stood still. The exact details have since been released from my soul and mind.

I never saw the face of the man who assaulted me and held my daughter and me against our will. At some point during the rape, I reached out to feel his hair. Maybe I was looking for something to identify him by? I am still not sure. Later I remember wondering if I would have a fear of all men.

After raping me, he took food from my refrigerator and then turned on all the water faucets in my house. I was frozen in fear.

I wanted to get up and call someone for help, but I couldn't move. When I finally made the phone call my friend was in disbelief; she called the police.

At the hospital check-in desk, I remember the officers using the word 'rape' and the staff chanting, 'alleged rape'. The **voice** in my mind was screaming, *how could you say that?* The nurses monologued about gathering DNA for evidence. There were some papers to sign – it was a blur. I felt **coerced** into putting my feet into stirrups and spreading my legs for them. Didn't they know I was already broken? Where were the compassion and humanity? I just wanted to be swaddled up with blankets and melt.

'The mother', as I referred to her, was called and she picked me up from the hospital. I guess someone had to. She took me out to a restaurant. No lie. I went into the bathroom and curled up in the corner on the floor. I wanted to stay there, but unfortunately, she came and escorted me to the dining room. I wondered how she could be so callous, so blind! I was still wearing the clothes I wore to the hospital, and I didn't even get the chance to shower. Not that I felt I could ever be clean again.

I could not stay at my condo. When I walked in, I felt sick so I went to a small cottage by the shore. The beach became my respite while I scrutinized every moment of the violent crime. I walked the beach deep in thought, not in the moment, **deeply wounded**. Sunrises, sunsets – hard liquor at night to ease the pain. *Why? Why me? Why did the hospital staff chant 'alleged' rape?*

There were moments where I cried out loud. Moments where I screamed and pounded my fists into the sand. I was numb, confused, and in pain. Thoughts tumbled in my mind like laundry in the dryer. I have since come to understand that it takes time and stillness to process a traumatic experience.

During my first stages of healing, I became aware of my extraordinary intuition. That insight strengthened as Spirit taught me to quiet my brain. I learned about love, wisdom, and forgiveness through omniscient communication. How do I explain the spirit realm to someone? There was a knowing inside of me, a power unexplainable. Perhaps best explained Carl Jung (1921), defined intuition as "perception via the unconscious". This power led me to heal myself and ultimately to be a healer. This was my journey. Each ocean wave a reminder that every moment holds an opportunity to live, to breathe, and to heal. We all have the power to heal ourselves. Each in our own way, and our own time.

I began meditation and yoga and had regular shiatsu massages. Through Spirit, I received intuitive messages, sometimes in the form of a flashing image. Other times they came in the form of a color, a sound or a feeling. As the messages became more vigorous, I saw pictures in my mind's eye, occasionally out of focus. The more my mind remained quiet, the clearer I could see and hear. My understanding of energy grew. We are entirely made of energy, and we are all self-healing. Learning to tune into our body energy and spirit takes a quiet mind and focused intent. The power of inner peace and finding stillness in your life influences the way you see the world and feel about yourself.

"Meditation can help us embrace our worries, our fear,
our anger; and that is very healing. We let our own
natural capacity of healing do the work."

- Thich Nhat Hanh

A significant shift occurred: I sold my business, moved to another state, and studied massage therapy. I found a midwife, became an apprentice and developed an insatiable appetite for herbal healing, natural living, and natural cooking books. My journey as a healer began with myself and broadened to serve those who seek a natural approach to wellness. Take a few moments here. Put down this book and breathe intentionally, allow your breath to become deeper. Let your abdomen rise with the inhale and fall with the exhale. Think about a time in your life when you made a shift.

As I tuned in to my inner self, nature became my medicine. I spent much time in the woods, thinking of them as walking meditations. As I began, I would set an intention and ask for nature to show me signs. I often biked, and cross-country skied.

One cold winter morning out cross-country skiing with friends, I got into a rhythm, and I was in the lead. I was overcome with an incredible pain – likened to a wire wrapped around my pelvis. It just kept getting tighter. Suddenly, the snow turned an intense indigo color, and I felt an energy surge through my whole body. It started at my feet and worked its way up my legs, into my pelvis, torso, and through my head. I felt weak, but then suddenly, the pain went away. Skiing allowed my mind to enter a state, much like the one you experience as you drift off to sleep. My intuition opened, and I received healing.

Being a rape victim created blockages in my energy field and shut down my chakras. They were closed and out of alignment. Becoming intrinsically aware of my breakthrough allowed them to heal. Intellectually processing psychic information released my sensuality, sexuality, and spirit.

I had an inherent knowledge of childbirth, herbal medicine, sensuality, and natural living. My healing energy was fortifying as I learned to trust the guidance I received. Through massage for clients and my hands-on approach, I intuitively knew physical things about them. A powerful experience was feeling the energy of a new pregnancy before the mother had confirmed it. I felt some of my clients' physical and spiritual wounds. I could see energy patterns inside their energy systems.

I would clear myself every morning and meditate. I attempted journaling, but had a way to go to become consistent. I made an effort to be gentle with myself as I acknowledged my feelings and emotions. My openness and trust allowed the information to become more powerful. The more that I shared myself, the deeper the healing.

I was called by Spirit to spend a month at the yoga ashram. The facility was formerly a monastery, and the sacred essence remained. The simplistic accommodations helped me to be at peace. Every morning, I meditated and then took a long walk outside. This was followed by a simple Ayurvedic breakfast, karma yoga, and more time in silence.

Group sessions of chanting, traditional tabla drumming, and Indian Harmonium lifted me to a higher spiritual level. I began seeing auras and recognizing energy patterns. In a conference with the Ayurvedic doctor and spiritual leaders of the ashram, I learned about self and depth of love. My physical energy was renewed; my mind had been reset to a blissful state of being. I returned home filled with gratitude, a limber body, and a new understanding of inner peace and healing.

Driving to work some time later, Spirit spoke and told me to go to college. I said out loud, "God if this you, you have the wrong car. I have a good job. I am satisfied. Life is good." Nevertheless, shortly after I was at the registration desk of the local community college. I thought I was to become a nurse and then a certified midwife. I sent away for my G.E.D. certificate and registered for classes.

I was juggling family, business, and now school so I quickly became worn out. After a day off from my thriving massage center, I returned to find an invite to a women's retreat. I made a phone call and accepted the invite.

A morning kundalini yoga session flowed into a discussion with the two Sikh teachers. They proposed a walk around town. It was then I learned of a low residency college where I could finish my degree. The teachers urged me to complete the process.

Another year passed. I was relaxing on the front porch with family and friends one summer evening when the phone rang. The caller ID said Connecticut Attorney General's Office. The voice on the line asked several questions, confirming I was the person they were looking for. They were calling with information pertaining to my rape and kidnapping. I was in disbelief – twenty years had passed. Time stood still. *Have they found my assailant? Were they able to make a DNA connection from the tests they put me through?* They reported that my assailant was issued the first 'John Doe arrest warrant' in Connecticut. This is an arrest warrant for an individual whose name is unknown. They are only known by DNA left at a crime scene.

I spent the rest of the night in shock, a heartbreaking setback. Layers of battle wounds were reopened, but life is like that. Life is a path and a process. We experience trauma so we can learn about our strengths, our purpose, and ourselves. We need to remember that we are free to choose our response to all types of experiences. We can choose the ordinary response and act like a victim, or we can choose to go within and find our strength. We open ourselves to alternative possibilities.

When morning broke, I got up and drove to Vermont to college. I arrived and was enthusiastic about starting my first low residency semester to complete my bachelor's degree. However, I found it difficult to concentrate and stay in the present. My mind kept wandering to the sexual violence. I came to understand I was in the next stage of my healing process. I made a choice to trust myself and continue on my healing journey I knew that with each day, as I tuned in on my study I was learning about myself, and my resilience. I was learning about my passion and my ability to dig deep. I was learning about gratitude and healing.

Time passed.

Somehow, when you have been through a traumatic experience, your body remembers it on a cellular level. It is difficult to describe.

Even though my body remembers what I've been through, I have taken a stand and found a life on the other side of trauma. I am strong. This brought a wellspring of resilience that I never knew I had. In many ways, it is a gift I never asked for.

My healing included unconditional forgiveness for my assailant. An inspirational author, Dan Zadra reminds us, 'Always know in your heart that you are far bigger than anything that can happen to you'. That is an amazing mantra to be repeated, written and remembered. Ultimately being full of gratitude for those on our path as well as the lessons we are here to learn is an important step on your healing journey.

My steadiness and effectiveness as a healer continue to develop. I refused to allow myself to be defined as a rape victim. From inconceivable victimization, I found my way through self-healing to become a woman that is strong, confident, and filled with gratitude. My story is uniquely my own.

We all have a story. How do we heal? How do we connect with Spirit and take a stand? I have experienced the full spectrum of negativity. It has been a powerful journey of opening up to the guidance of spirituality and healing myself.

Have you ever been in a situation of terrorizing fear? The deep-seated type that interrupts your sleep, and causes you to be irritable and have trouble concentrating. You may have been surrounded by happy people who appear confident and balanced. Were you able to make a shift?

What is your response to fear? When you are experiencing **fear**, is it hard to see through the veil? You have to find a way to reach and heal the wound in your heart. When there is anguish inside of you that won't go away, a powerful yet simple practice is deep breathing to center yourself. Centering yourself literally means bringing your awareness to your center or stomach area. Through breathing, you will recognize that fear is a tight energy in your body. You will learn that you have the power to change it into a positive energy.

Are there relationships in your life where you feel your **voice** isn't heard? As a human being you have a deep desire to be heard. Speak your truth first through journaling for self-awakening and a means to heal emotional wounds. You must be honest and uncensored. You will unearth emotional truth through the layers. You simply open up and write from your heart. Learn to write and speak positive, 'I am _____'messages.

Are you being **coerced**? Is there someone in your life who overwhelms your will by force? Breaking this cycle can be one of the most difficult. Many are unable to rise above without assistance. There is much help available. The first step is to ask for help if you need it. We can be **deeply wounded** in so many ways. A foundation of healing can be built on the premise of refusing to be defined by your victim mentality. Whatever harm has come to you can be used as a challenge to overcome this mentality. This is an opportunity to find your inner strength and practice unconditional forgiveness and compassion.

The journey to self-healing can be the most difficult challenge of your life. But it will also be the most precious gift you will give yourself and the world. There will be seemingly insurmountable challenges and blocks along the way. Believe in yourself!

Bethany Kelly

Bethany Kelly is a momma to three kids, a wife, and an English teacher. Her faith in God and love of writing have helped her to move on from past trauma, allowing her to change her mindset from victim to resilient survivor.

She holds a Bachelor of Arts in English and a Master of Fine Arts in Creative Writing, equipping her with the tools that she needs to share her love of the written word with others. A long-time writer and therapeutic writing enthusiast, Bethany aspires to help others work through their pain, one word at a time.

Chapter 12

Lord, I Give You Control

By Bethany Kelly

When I walked into the house, the screen door slammed shut. The smell of alcohol was so strong that I couldn't help but wonder how long they had been drinking before we had gotten there. I didn't really want to drink anything, but I took the red Dixie cup when Logan gave it to me.

"So…where is everyone?" I asked, seeing only a few boys in the house. I didn't know all of them, but I was pretty sure that they were all Logan's cousins.

"We're it, sweet pea," one of the boys responded. "Drink up." I took a sip of my drink and did my best to keep a straight face as the vodka burned a trail down my throat and into my belly.

Logan sat down on a worn couch and patted the spot next to him. "Come sit, babe." I walked over to the couch and sat down next to him, noticing the way he possessively put his arm around me and pulled me closer.

We weren't even dating…at least he had yet to ask me. We had been texting and hanging out for a few weeks. He had even taken me to a football game a few weeks prior. However, anytime I asked him what it was that we were doing, I was met with silence. I quickly learned not to ask that question and just enjoy the time that I got to spend with him. He was, after all, one of the most popular boys at his school.

"Whatcha thinkin' about?" Logan's question tore me out of my thoughts.

"Oh, just zonin'." I smiled up at him and set my drink down on the coffee table. Logan picked it up and handed it back to me.

"You haven't even finished a glass, yet. Don't tell me you're already done." I didn't want the guys to think I was a wuss, especially Logan, so I downed the rest of the vodka and got up to throw the cup in the trash.

When I turned around to head back to the couch, Logan was behind me. He reached his hand up to my cheek and caressed it, pulling me closer to him. When he kissed me, my world stopped. This was my first 'intense' kiss, and I couldn't believe that I was having it with Logan. Then the whooping and hollering began, and I felt myself coming back to reality.

"Logan, not here," I said, pulling away from him.

"Ooooo…better get her to a room before she cools down." One of Logan's cousins was opening the door to what I could only assume was a bedroom.

"Want to go hang out by ourselves for a while?" he asked. Before I could answer, he grabbed my arm and guided me to the room. I began to feel nervous. Yes, we had been alone in his truck before, but this was different. I had never had sex before, and I wasn't planning on it, yet. He shut the door behind us and walked me over to a mattress in the corner of the room. The bedspread on it was old and tattered, the ugly floral design hard to discern.

We sat down on the bed and again, he kissed me. His hand began to wander, tracing the side of my bra, moving closer to the front of my body. I moved his hand away from my chest and up to my face. Did I want to be kissing him? Yes. Did I want anything else? I wasn't sure. I hardly knew him, and I had been told since I was little to wait for the right person. To wait until I was married.

"Help me out here," he said as he lifted the bottom of my shirt up. I left my arms where they were. Would he get the message? He lightly lifted my arms up. Obviously not. I stopped kissing him and scooted over to the other side of the bed.

"Can we just cuddle?" I asked, like an idiot.

"Sure, babe." He lay down on the bed and put his arm out for me to come spoon with him. I laid down next to him, and the first thing that he did was unbutton my jeans, quickly putting his hand beneath my undergarment. I didn't make a sound. Didn't move. Didn't do anything for a few seconds. Finally, as he went farther and farther down, I sat up.

"Stop," I said.

He took his hand out of my pants and sat up, frowning. "What's up? You don't like it?"

"No," I answered quietly. He pushed me down onto the bed and yanked my pants off.

I remember telling him to stop several times. This wasn't what I wanted. I just wanted to be accepted. To have fun. To have a boyfriend. I didn't want this. I didn't want to leave the bedroom feeling dirty. I didn't want the catcalls that I got when he led me to his truck. I definitely didn't want to sit in the shower, scrubbing my skin until it felt like it was burning. I didn't want to lose my innocence to a guy who only wanted one thing…and it wasn't 'forever'.

I watched as the crimson blood slowly made its way down to the drain, pooling around the edges instead of accepting its fate. One more cut. This time a little deeper. My arm began to tingle, and I dropped the razor blade in the sink. I quickly got a piece of toilet paper and dabbed at the blood collecting on my arm.

My heart was hammering in my chest. It did every time I cut. Even though I felt better…more in control, I was also ashamed. Ashamed that I had to rely on something so pathetic to keep me behaving normally in public.

Breathe, Bethany. Blood always made me squeamish.

After a few minutes of pressure on the cut, I got the liquid bandage from the cabinet and opened it. I winced as I painted it on my cuts. It was almost beautiful…the lines latticing up my arm like a design only rivaled by the most excellent of craftsmen.

I pulled my sleeves down over my handiwork and rejoined my family. *If only they knew everything happening on my body and in my mind. Would they be as ashamed as I am?*

When Mom took me to my favorite Chinese restaurant, I should've known it was a set-up as soon as she picked me up to go. After we got our egg drop soup, she gave me *the look*. Every mom has one; a look that could make a priest shudder and worry about what was about to happen.

"Show me your arms," she said. I never really liked how blunt and straightforward she was; even less so now. I slowly lifted up my sleeves, ashamed of what she was about to see. I could see the tears begin to form in her eyes as she took in the sight of the handiwork I had just been so proud of.

"I'm sorry, Momma," I mumbled.

"We just went over this with Kate. You said you would never do that. You said you would never hurt yourself!" I started pulling on the rubber band around my wrist and letting go of it, trying to keep my thoughts under control. Trying to keep my impulses under control.

By this time, I had been cutting daily for a few months. What my mom couldn't see were the cuts that littered the bottom of my feet, my stomach, and my hands. I had run out of room on my arms, and I had almost been caught a few times, so I hadn't cut my arms in over a week. What Mom was seeing were cuts that had already begun to heal.

I honestly don't remember the rest of that meal. I just remember the shame that I felt; not shame at the fact that I had cut myself, but shame at the fact that I had let Mom find out. I didn't want her having to stress over this. This was my habit. My way of handling everything. It wasn't supposed to be her problem, too.

Although I continued to cut after Mom figured out my secret, I made sure they were smaller and in places that she wouldn't look. I became obsessed with finding places on my body that I could harm. Places that I could make a precise, tiny incision that caused a lot of pain, but that wasn't normally exposed. In between my toes became the premier destination.

Between my shame from Logan and the shame of cutting, I began to have a skewed vision of my self-worth. All I wanted was to feel normal again. I didn't want my life to revolve around one night. Every time I looked in the mirror, all I saw were flaws, cuts, blemishes, and imperfections. My chest was too small. My tummy was too big. He had taken all of the features I used to see as beautiful and turned them into the many grains of sand that made up the punching bag I had turned myself into.

I was almost at my lowest when I met Andrew – whom I didn't know had a wife and kids. He was nine years older than I was, but he gave me the kind of attention that I craved. He not only brought me wildflowers and flirted with me every time he had the chance, but he also gave me an escape. When I was with him, I didn't feel damaged or dirty.

Unfortunately, that didn't last long. He became possessive, and like Logan, he wanted more than I could give. But by then, I just didn't care. I had checked out of my life. I went through the motions, but I was no longer truly living.

I let him leave bruises on me. I let him yell at me and convince me that I was worthless. Most of the time, I really thought that I was worthless. I believed that Logan took all of my worthiness and that all I deserved was to be used and harmed, which is what I let him do to me.

Andrew had an issue of his own. His wife found out about me, and she was furious. He quit working in the same town as me, and I was free. But I didn't feel free. I was just lonely. That is until I met my husband.

One night we drove to the park together and went back to an area that looked like an old-fashioned town. There were a bunch of one-room buildings, a school, several houses, and a church. We sat on a swing on one of the porches that was in front of the houses. We hadn't been hanging out for very long. However, I could already tell that I didn't ever want to let him go.

He didn't pressure me into anything. He was sweet, and he didn't mind falling asleep on the phone with me. He combated my nightmares, and I began to slow down on cutting myself. That wasn't how I always felt about him though…

When I first met him, I did not like him at all…and he didn't like me. But we did have something in common…we knew what it was like to feel like nothing. Eventually, we bonded over that, and we became each other's confidants. I made him feel worthy, and he made me feel worthy.

"Hear the crickets?" he asked.

"Mhm," I replied, smiling at him. I was sitting on his lap, resting my head on his shoulder.

"Crickets are supposed to be lucky, right?"

"I guess so." I had always been told that crickets were supposed to bring good luck, but I didn't like bugs of any kind…even crickets.

"If crickets are lucky, then maybe…you'll be my girlfriend." He didn't exactly pose it as a question. Instead, he seemed to be musing about the possibility that I would say yes.

"Yeah," I said. "I'd love to."

That was the moment that he saved me. Not just from a possessive man who came back to claim me, but from myself. He was the only person who kept me from going off the deep end. When Andrew showed up at my job and had to be pulled off of me by my manager, he was there, comforting me right after it happened. He gave me Tylenol for the pain and frozen vegetables for the bruises. When he saw me sinking back into that hole of depression and self-loathing, he brought me back.

Ever since I was a teenager, he's kept me focused on God. He's kept me focused on all of the blessings that I have in my life. He taught me how to be grateful for what I have, instead of angry because of what I've had to go through to get to where I'm at.

After Logan took what I thought was my worth, I went into a downward spiral. Sure, I kept my grades up and seemed fine on the outside, but bubbling underneath the surface was shame, anger, sadness, and a whole bunch of other emotions that I can't even begin to describe.

However, if Logan hadn't of taken me to that room, I wouldn't be the person I am now. I wouldn't have the relationship that I now have with God. I wouldn't have gotten to experience the love that I experience today with my wonderful husband. I wouldn't be as equipped to help the kids that I come into contact with on a daily basis. I wouldn't have those life experiences to be able to relate to them and caution them away from bad decisions.

Something that I have to remind myself of every day is that God turns every bad thing into something good.

No one's memories are crystal-clear. My memories are frayed by the experiences I have gone through. It's strange what small details stick out to you when you look back on things.

My memories of that night are based on my recollection of what happened after my innocence was taken from me. I am sure that when I was in the moment, I thought the small gathering was fun. I'm sure that I felt Logan really cared for me. Honestly, that night probably seemed like a night I would never forget...not because I was about to be raped, but because I was with one of the most popular guys in town.

After I threw myself down because I felt like I deserved it, I had nowhere else to go but up. I began to not only lean on God's word, but I also gave up control to Him. Cutting myself was about having control over something, even if it was something unhealthy. Letting a man abuse me was about control because I felt that I deserved to be treated that way. I found the answer to all of my control issues by giving it all to God. He told me clearly that He would take care of me...and I believed Him. Everything that happened from that point forward, I welcomed, because I knew it was being controlled by God.

God doesn't promise that bad things won't happen to us. He promises that He will be thulere with us – and for us – when we are in the midst of those bad things. If you are struggling with abuse, sexual assault, depression, self-harm, control issues, etc., please give your problems to God. He can handle anything, and He will turn everything bad into something good.

And we know that God causes everything to work together for the good of those who love God and are called according to His purpose for them.

- Romans 8:28

Maryann Kelly

Following a successful thirty-three-year corporate career working globally, Maryann has earned certifications in advanced medical intuition, Light Grid, and Reiki in addition to her university degrees. She's also completed spiritual mediumship programs and the Donna Eden Online Energy Medicine Curricula.

She's the founder of Intuitive Services LLC, providing medium, mentorship, and speaking services.

Maryann's unique combination of hands-on health care, business, and holistic experience enables her to help clients connect with loved ones that have passed over; obtain insights about health, and apply intuition in business. Maryann delivers services with the highest integrity and compassion for her clients.

Find Maryann online:

Websites: http://intuitiveservicesinsight.com
Facebook: https://www.facebook.com/Intuitive-Services-136719273750619/

Chapter 13

The Thunder of Intuition

By Maryann Kelly

"What, is this all there is?" This was the recurring question that began in grammar school. This question had a pulse like a tap of thunder that I heard and felt viscerally from my core. New school subjects, family, and friends were distractions from this question. My grandmother became ill starting when I was ten years old. During her four-year illness, I had spent more time with her. I hadn't understood the things she was telling me about the future during our long talks, but somewhere down deep inside my adolescent being, I was positive that she knew that no, this is not all there is. There is so much more.

My appetite for knowledge across school subject areas was insatiable. However, financial pressures and the reality of having to figure out a way to pay for college and support myself was of paramount importance, so I focused on practical subjects. I was grateful to be able to excel in the curricula while I worked in clinical roles during high school and university. As I had performed my clinical duties, I began to identify patient issues quickly and accurately before the physicians had arrived.

However, I said nothing as I was still attributing this to my scholastic aptitude. Open-heart surgeries were performed at an increasing pace as technology and techniques were improved. However, I had promised myself at eighteen years – as I witnessed more and more middle-aged patients go through this extremely invasive surgery – that this would not happen to me. I would take care of myself.

I recalled my grandmother passing over, and I had seen more people pass over in the hospital, so I didn't feel the grief of finality that was expected and that burdened others. I felt their peace and movement onwards. I really felt like I didn't fit in, a feeling that was to become an ever-increasing reality. Again, I didn't talk about this as it could be perceived as cold and insensitive regarding the loss of a loved one. But that was just it, I was feeling *more*, not less. It wasn't a feeling of such finality, it was a continuance. While intrigued by my different reaction to death, I maintained my course to control as much as I could by working hard, getting good grades, and securing a corporate job. I went through university as a double major in two years and eight months. While working and juggling bus schedules I graduated Summa Cum Laude. I began a coveted position in a prestigious firm. So far, this control mantra was working out just fine, and I just had to complete the checklist for security, success and happiness. This is what we are taught. I thought if I just did everything I was meant to, that I could fit in and feel safe, secure and loved.

Fast-forward more than thirty years across many job promotions and awards. I was often the go-to person for the highest-level executives. I could determine what I had thought were obscure root causes of problems and devise creative solutions. While I was always grateful for such recognition, the high that I saw others experience in similar circumstances lasted for weeks, months, or years - whereas my high lasted days. That tap of thunder I spoke of earlier had increased to a hum, and then was significantly upgraded to an internal vibration with a predictable cadence that was triggered by specific events. I knew I had everything to be grateful for, and I was indeed grateful. However, gratitude was not soothing this constant disruptive vibration. I used my surgically induced menopause, the 2008 credit crisis, and the sudden death of my sister and a beloved friend as some of the reasons for this nagging vibration that dug a bigger void and left me more unsettled. After all, I was a professional who valued facts and control. I had been at the top of my game in my career, and all the facts pointed to what's defined as fulfillment. So, imagine my surprise when I ended up in an emergency room in my mid-fifties with chest pain!

When I had slowed down to heed the warning my emergency room visit provided, that internal vibration was a force not to be ignored. While I still didn't have an answer that I could articulate to the question, 'What, is this all there is?', I knew that I was suffocating while continuing the same pattern. The vibration was so heavy and negative that regardless of status and society's expectations, I had to take my own self-appointed desired detour to figure this out. To have more flexibility, I did consulting work. While in the emergency room, I had made and assessed my bucket list. I wasn't going to postpone things anymore.

Having never had a hobby, I tried a couple of neighborhood art classes and took a free ballroom dance lesson. A friend, who was a fact-based business woman like me, had told me about her unplanned interaction with a spiritual medium who blew her mind, given the accuracy and specific detail. I was extremely skeptical, but curious, so I went to see this spirit medium. I was stunned like never before as he relayed specifics that only I could know. I continued business-consulting, artwork, and increased my focus on the mediumship process and ballroom dancing. Unlike when I had begun to learn other new topics related to science, mathematics, languages, technology or business – learning about mediumship and ballroom dancing was fulfilling in ways that could not begin to compare with decades of past achievements.

Within months of first seeing the spirit medium, he casually informed me that I could do what he was doing in communicating with those passed over. I was in disbelief. He asked if I wanted to find out, so I said sure. I quieted my mind in the way we discussed during past visits. He put three pictures in front of me of individuals I had never seen before, and a flood of information came to me.

When I saw the first picture, I said that this man had been in World War II, fixing airplane engines on aircraft carriers in the Navy. He had married twice. He hadn't seen his children as much as he should have, especially since his second marriage. He had died of respiratory failure in Florida. I was informed that all of this was correct!

When I saw the second picture, I said that this man hadn't completed as much of higher education as his intellect would have allowed. He had not married. He taught a specialized subject to children out of his home. His house was two stories, with an external staircase from the second floor to the first floor. His death involved blunt force trauma. I was informed that all of this was also correct and that the specialized subject taught to children out of his home was music.

When I saw the third picture, I said that the young man was a sweet person who, during his young life, had been struggling horribly with demons associated with drug addiction. He was between worlds. I was informed that this information was again correct, and that the person had been in and out of a coma.

Part of me was wondering who was speaking as I heard all this detail stated. Then I realized that I was speaking. This information was playing like a movie in my head that I was narrating. When he told me that I had gotten so many of the details correct, (something that often takes others a lifetime to be able to tap into), I was speechless, and I've *never* been speechless. At that moment, I realized that I had felt a peace and calm like never before. The vibration was stronger than ever from head to toe, it was soothing. The now roaring thunder of intuitive knowledge resonated and was shared more instantaneously from the pictures of these individuals, faster than anything else I had experienced. The persistent question was answered quite unexpectedly and suddenly on a Sunday afternoon.

Now, in my fifties, I finally know the answer to the persistent question, 'What, is this all there is?' The answer is that no, this is not all there is. There is so much more, and that 'more' can be tapped into from anywhere on earth! While this may sound similar to faith or religion (I had many years of training in such), this, for me, is different because of the details that came through me. I was mesmerized that I could relay such specific detail about the individuals from just seeing their pictures. Previously, my experience with applying my own intuition had occurred during some private moments with my grandmother, during my time in clinical roles identifying patients' issues before the physician diagnosis, and during incidents in business identifying obscure root causes that created issues. My retrospective yielded a perspective acknowledging these seemingly disparate experiences as all being part of my intuition. So, what do I do now? I asked myself what happens with four decades of work experience? Essentially, I kept quiet until I could figure this out as people would think I was crazy, and I wouldn't blame them for thinking that.

Within days of this epiphany, I was trying ballroom dancing. Within a few lessons with my truly wonderful ballroom dance instructors, Eugene LaPierre and Jonathan Cabrera, another very strange development happened. I was having fun, but there was a kind of energy exchange happening that seemed to fuel my abilities in mediumship.

The scientist in me ran experiments of course. Yes, the correlation was repeatedly undeniable. The more I did ballroom dancing with these specific people, the more my abilities developed. The additional revelation was that I, the type A+++ workaholic control freak, was in control of nothing! I had to wait and follow the lead in every dance when I have been used to leading my entire life and setting the pace. The more I pushed to develop in mediumship, the more I had to wait. I was more vulnerable than ever and also, paradoxically, felt transcendent with joy like never before.

Finally, while I could not wrap words around these experiences, there was an internal truth surfacing. Addressing this internal truth is necessary and certainly has an invaluable upside, but working on yourself is the hardest and most humbling task ever, one that's full of surprising twists and turns. One moment of truth was that, without conscious thought, I found myself literally running as soon as I was outside of a building where I had declined a six-figure job. Being vulnerable was the easy part. Next was waiting, more waiting, and waiting again until I got to the next stages of trust and surrender!

I panicked because I wanted to figure this out fast, and on my timeline, as I had always done. I read voraciously on a wide variety of topics related to mediumship, such as metaphysics and spirituality. I also had the now laughable notion that I could read my way to dancing better, faster. I had my patient mentors Rich Braconi and Lisa O'Brien, along with my dance instructors Eugene LaPierre and Jonathan Cabrera, who kept informing me that neither mediumship nor ballroom dancing works this way. Eventually, I kept learning and will continue to learn what trust and surrender really mean. The more I trusted and surrendered and stopped trying to force things to happen on my terms, the more my mediumship and ballroom dance abilities developed. This has been the most difficult and the most rewarding work. Now, to be able to offer closure or peace via readings to connect with loved ones, or to offer helpful health information and then see the look on people's faces transform is an amazing feeling. To mentor someone in business so that they can tap into their own intuition for their work helps that person as well as those around them.

During my self-assigned detour, I met all kinds of amazing people whom I would never have met had I stayed in my controlled course. University students at the ballroom adopted me as their ballroom mom, which is a role I cherish. The work I did on myself healed deep wounds. The work I continue to do keeps me humble and grounded in applying intuition in mediumship and mentoring, and staying grounded happens to be a core principal in ballroom dance as well. The art lessons I had taken early in the detour are now applied as I offer soul portraits from readings for clients. The fear that I had had about letting go and about what will others think is gone. I am a better person now. My life is much richer in ways that cannot be monetized. While many people from my previous fifty years were surprised and may not have understood my new work, their encouragement was so appreciated.

I could have never predicted this transformation. I am delighted to say that both of my mentors, ballroom dance instructors, and two additional wonderful women, Bernadette Spector and Raye LaValley, stuck with me during this journey, which warrants high praise for them. I was not the easiest person to be around sometimes, as I desperately tried to figure out what was happening. At a venue where I work, I get to see a former co-worker, M. Marcinko, who has helped me significantly, on a regular basis.

The person who stood by me as Amazon orders showed up with the most unusual items, including ballroom shoes, metaphysics books, and crystals was my ever patient and devoted husband. The depths of his love and support made this fabulous journey possible. I am so blessed.

It's worth listening to your intuition! Happiness and fulfillment can have very different criteria when compared to society standards. I made my intuition intentional by listening and then taking the corresponding action!

Since my epiphany, I have been so grateful for the opportunity to help others personally or in business along their journey. How may I help you on your journey?

Shilamida Kupershteyn

Shilamida Kupershteyn is a licensed acupuncturist, spiritual guide, healthy living mentor and bestselling author of *31 Days of Gratitude-Create the Life You Desire - an interactive gratitude journal.*

After making six figures, she experienced a succession of disasters and unforeseen circumstances that led her to poverty and panic. She credits over a decade of spiritual studies alongside the world's foremost spiritual leaders, with helping her to gain a sense of empowerment and create the life she desired. Now, Shilamida works with people to help them realize their dreams and create the life they desire through the law of attraction and manifestation.

Find Shilamida online:

Website: www.Shilamida.com
Facebook group: http://www.facebook.com/groups/
                 Shilamidainspires
Facebook page: www.Facebook.com/shilamida

Chapter 14

●

Believe in Yourself and
Magic Will Happen

By Shilamida Kupershteyn

Let me paint you a picture of my story. As a single mother paying my way through acupuncture school, every penny counted. I depended on child support and I collected coupons from neighbors for food so I could scrape enough money to pay my rent every month. I would eat subway sandwiches for an entire week due to their special coupons for breakfast options and $1.99 foot long sandwiches for lunch and dinner.

Prior to finding out I was pregnant, my father passed away. My ex never asked his permission for my hand in marriage, so we were separated by the time I discovered I was pregnant. I lay in his bed crying for hours, wishing for death myself, wishing for it to be me with an awful disease. I was devastated and broken in so many ways. How could I be pregnant? How could I own a business I hated? How did I get here? Two months after my father's passing I made the final decision to break it off completely with my ex. How was it possible that I would find out I was pregnant after that, and allow this relationship to continue?

During my pregnancy, I gained 100 lbs. I was sad, depressed, and self-conscious from the added weight. I despised myself and loathed looking in the mirror. No form of fad diet or weight loss pill was working. I even attended an Overeaters Anonymous meeting. It seemed hopeless; I felt doomed and never thought I would be happy again.

One day when my son was about nine months old, a new friend came over to my house. As I sat complaining about my relationship, my weight, and life, she started talking about the law of attraction. Her energy was so positive, upbeat, and awakening. This was a feeling I have never experienced or at least never paid attention to. Her advice to me was to learn about the *The Secret*, that it would change my life.

The very day she left, I purchased the DVD. As I started watching and heard about the law of attraction, it occurred to me this wasn't the first time I heard this term. Back when I was twenty-one, I worked at a multi-level marketing company. I met a woman in the conference room who had also told me I needed to read about it.

That evening, upon returning home, I walked into my bedroom. There, on my shelf was a copy of the book, covered with seven years' worth of dust. For seven years, that very book traveled with me unread. I had been in possession of the very secret that would change my life forever. The secret to my happiness.

In many ways, the words in the book aligned with the movie. This all reinforced the fact that I needed a change. I was eager and ready to begin. In the movie, it said to create a vision board and keep a journal. I purchased a board at my local store and ordered a journal online.

I desired to explore the world, so half the board was covered with travel. My previous work accomplishments were successful, but nothing lasted. So on the other half, I put my desire to be a motivational speaker and an author. The anxiety returned. What was I motivating people to do, and who would listen to a 'nobody' like me?

I turned to the universe for guidance. I asked for help to find the right path, my path. To please help me find and fulfill my purpose. My ideal success would be on stage, telling my story and motivating others. I was ready and open to receive. The burning fire ignited within me to make these changes. It was at that very moment my belief and life began.

It was on December 28th, 2008, I ended my toxic relationship with my son's father. I was riddled with anxiety, terror, and fear. Yet, I *still* knew somehow that it would be ok. One week later, I made an appointment with a psychic. Ironically, it was a gift my ex had given me for Christmas. It had been years since I went to one because while my father was ill, I did not want anyone to deliver fatal news. For this appointment, I remained open-minded. I will reveal some of what happened, so you have some idea of my experience.

I sat before her, only revealing my name. As she handed me the deck of cards she said, "Hold the cards, and in your mind's eye, and ask them a question." I asked myself, *Did I make the right decision by leaving my son's dad?* She flipped the first card and said, "You made the right decision, he's not the right guy for you." Whoa! I was blown away! Then she flipped the second card and said, "Is there anyone from the other side that you want to connect with? I am a medium." I said maybe. She replied, "Well your father is coming through." I started to sweat, my heart began racing...was she serious? Could she really talk to my dad? I missed him so much. I wanted to see him, talk to him, and feel him.

She started describing him to me. Every detail was spot on. Then she told me that I would be very successful and that my dad was very proud of the mom that I became. She said that my son was destined for greatness. He had a special gift and he would turn to me to develop it, because I had the same one!

What? I was an event planner. What the heck did I know? I didn't have a gift. Maybe I had the gift of decorating a good party, or the gift of sales, but those weren't really *gifts*, were they? When the session ended, I was floored. I experienced a strange feeling that I didn't understand. While I was standing in the mystical shop with my emotions stirring, I decided to purchase a CD/book on chakras, a deck of angel cards by Doreen Virtue, and a candle. While I had no idea what I was feeling at that moment, it was to be the first day of the rest of my life.

The following day I was with my mother at the plastic surgeon's office. She was battling cancer for the second time. As I was waiting, listening to my chakra CD and reading the book, I glanced at her face and saw how sad she was. She did not want to lose her breasts. My heart broke; I assured her that it would be ok. A body part did not define her beauty, and she was loved regardless. This was another awakening that told me I still was not on my path. I needed to help people.

After my father passed away, I contemplated going to nursing school, but I knew that wasn't my calling. I decided to enroll in massage school in the hope of meeting other people on my wavelength and making spiritual connections. At the time, I did not have any spiritual friends and had declared myself 'a crazy person'. Surely, on this path I could find similar personalities.

Three weeks into massage school, I decided I couldn't do this for the rest of my life. I loved it, but with my weight problems I was exhausted after every session. It was at that school that I learned about acupuncture and Reiki. Now, looking back, I realize the universe was putting me on my path.

A couple of weeks later we had a session on reflexology that I loved. I wanted to learn more, so I googled reflexology classes. I found a center that was hosting a healing circle with a woman named Julia. The weekends that I did not have my son were hard! I was sad and cried a lot. I thought to myself, *Maybe I should go.* So I did. I showed up to this healing circle and did the exercises. When I left, I felt like 20 lbs of negativity was removed from my body. It was profound! That was my first introduction to the Americana Leadership College. This organization helped me through a lot of spiritual work and aided in my healing.

It was there I learned about forgiveness. Experiences in my early twenties evolved into my harboring a lot of anger. My success in one company was foiled by management, conveniently before bonus time to make it look like I was stealing information. The devastation of the accusation combined with the necessity of the monetary bonus due to credit card debt left me in a place of mental anguish. My integrity was attacked, my character was defamed, and I was angry. Then one day while stopped at a red light, I suddenly released a fierce scream and yelled, "I forgive you JG, for what you have done to me. I release you." Tears of relief streamed down my cheek. It was the moment I realized the importance of forgiveness and my life started to shift in the week that followed.

That very same week, after reconnecting with an old high school friend on Facebook, I was invited to his home for a mini-reunion. It was there that I met his wife. My first instinct was one of judgment. I did not care for her personality. She then sent me a friend request on Facebook. As to not be rude (despite my dislike), I accepted. Her intrusive questions began to disturb me, so I responded with one-word answers.

Some time later, in June, I was invited to another party at their home for their daughter's birthday. I had no plans, so I accepted the invitation. Upon arriving, I immediately saw that they were unprepared and in need of assistance. My event planner mode kicked in. Towards the end of the party, we were chatting, and the questions began again. I addressed her directly, asking why she continued to ask an abundance of questions. She revealed that she was an acupuncturist and was looking for a massage therapist for her office. She then asked when I could start. I was taken back by her thoughtfulness. As we continued to talk, I let her know that I was graduating in a week, and following that, I was going for surgery. She offered to come to my house to give me an acupuncture treatment post-surgery to help me heal faster. I was grateful for her kind gesture and so ashamed of myself for the judgment I had prior.

The day after my surgery, she came over as promised and gave me my treatment. It was amazing. Afterward, she lay on the bed with me and we started chatting. I was shocked, she was just as 'crazy' as I was! She believed the same things I did. I judged her because she was socially awkward and I was an extrovert. I must've seen myself within her, so I tried to separate myself instead of embracing her. This was my first true lesson on judgment. I almost disconnected from my soul sister because of my ego and my lack of the ability to be accepting of all. This lesson would play out for me many times in the year to come. As you read this, I hope you'll open up to see where your judgment lies and how you may be cutting yourself off from opportunities.

In the time we spent together, she told me that if I were on a spiritual journey then going to acupuncture school would change my life and help me with what I wanted to accomplish. I had no idea what I was getting into, but I called and made an appointment with the dean of the school. The dean asked me if I had any questions. I said no. He looked at me puzzled and said, "Are you sure?" I replied, "Yes." He thanked me for coming and sent me over to the bursar's office. The cost for three years of school in 2009 was $55,000. I was still in debt from massage school, and I had little to no money at that point. I felt unsure, so I spoke to my friend. "Just do it, you will make your money back. Take out loans, trust me," she said. Having no one to turn to and believing everyone would try to talk me out of it, I resorted to calling my ex. He laughed, telling me I was crazy, but that he would do his best to help me with our son.

The next year would prove to be the hardest of my life. I had a full-time school schedule; I was paying off debts, taking care of my son, dealing with emotions, and still facing attempts at weight loss. In the end, I started to see a shift. I started eating better, feeling better, and gained confidence in myself as an acupuncturist.

I really started manifesting what I wanted my life to look like. My body was changing, but more importantly, my mind was changing. I was dating a lot and feeling good about myself. On April 26th, 2007 I met my soul mate. For the first time in my life, I felt true unconditional love. Love that was so pure, and so amazing. This was the happiest I had ever been. From there, the pieces of my life started to come together. The next six years would be above and beyond my wildest dreams.

We now have five kids between the two of us, we had our youngest two together. We bought a beautiful house that we've turned into a loving home. I have a thriving acupuncture practice where I now earn six figures. I am a bestselling author on Amazon, a speaker, and a coach! All of my manifestations are coming true, and I get to spend my days helping people create the life they desire! Happiness, love, anything you want really, is at your reach! Believe in yourself, believe in the universe, and magic will happen!

Eugene LaPierre

Eugene a professional ballroom dancer/competitor; studio owner; head of a university ballroom program; and founder of a non-profit, called Ballroom Dancing For A Better U, has seen how ballroom dancing can enhance lives of children and adults. Eugene's ability to 'connect' allows others, regardless of demographics, challenges, health issues, or special needs to feel joy; have a voice that wasn't previously heard, and be valued as an equal.

Eugene's palpable compassion instills trust, resulting in improvements in cognitive, physical and social skills among those in geriatric communities or with varying special needs.

Find Eugene online:

Websites: http://www.lapierreballroom.com/
http://www.bd4bu.org/
Facebook: https://www.facebook.com/
LaPierreBallroomDanceStudio

Chapter 15

Altruism Alive: Lives Opened Wide

By Eugene LaPierre

Our world continually gets faster and faster due to technology. Increasing demands from many fronts invade any potential spare second, so more activities are multitasked. Who has time for altruism?

While I am absolutely for equality and thinking of the bigger picture for the greater good, an encounter with a local Dancing with the Stars (DWTS), production really opened my eyes. The lives of so many others involve so many different people, whereas my routine involved many of the same people. While my challenges were real, the challenges and everyday lives of others were more complex, involving a broader set of community programs and/or caring for children, elderly parents, and caring for those with physical and mental special needs. I had realized that my view of a community with equality that values the greater good was correct, but my exposure to what that really meant to my everyday life had been limited.

My situation was stable. I had suitable work providing an income sufficient to support my lifestyle. I was appreciative, as many don't have these basic requirements met. I worked hard, as consistent with my work ethic. However, the opportunity for further development and the autonomy of creative expression that I desired were not going to happen in my stable, comfortable situation. It was through a local DWTS program that I was introduced to someone new. In this conversation, an idea was suggested regarding my having my own ballroom dance studio, especially since a local venue was available for lease. In my late forties and after the 2008 credit crisis, did I want to risk so much and go out on my own, especially since ballroom dance studios rely on the discretionary income of clients who have time and want to spend money on learning how to ballroom dance in a finite geography? My creative process was now on a trajectory and speed akin to the space shuttle. (Who needs NASA?) Thoughts of the interior design of my studio displayed in my mind. Visions of choreography I had wanted to do danced in harmony with the classes and events I would have. The details that had annoyed me, I would address with excellence. And the people who could participate in ballroom dance programs that I would tailor for them and bring to them would include those so often left behind, left out, or not even considered. I would include tots, teens, tea tootlers or said another way, children, adolescents, adults and seniors (beverage preference of tea or not is optional). I would include all those with special mental and/or physical needs.

If I were out on my own, I could create my own non-profit as well with the mission that ballroom dancing can bring important positive changes in the lives of every individual. There has been growing evidence that shows that stimulating one's mind by dancing can ward off Alzheimer's disease and dementia, much like physical exercise can keep the body fit. Dancing also increases cognitive acuity at all ages. My goal is for *everyone* to have the opportunity of benefiting from ballroom dancing regardless of age, health limitations or economic status.

I weighed my current stability against the stagnation I had been feeling. I weighed my security against doing more for all as part of equality for a much larger part of the community. They may not be seen, but they are there. I risked everything, post-credit crisis, in ballroom dance work requiring clients to have and then choose to spend their discretionary income on my local ballroom dance services. I went into debt and opened a studio. While getting the studio up and running as a one-man operation, I found time to go to facilities to talk about how ballroom dancing can help the geriatric community and those with special needs. I met more like-minded people from all walks of life who infused encouragement. I got to know so many more whose daily lives inspired me as to all they could do and the many lives they touched. My definition of equality and community expanded exponentially. There was so much to be done, and that could be done. Without my non-profit, Ballroom Dancing For A Better U (BD4BU), started yet and without funds, I volunteered and worked with people at their facilities anyway. I saw the improvements in their social, physical, and mental abilities. I saw their smiles, which were small and tentative at first as they tried out this new ballroom dance experience. The smiles then included hugs. I felt their hugs become stronger as they embraced me longer. I silently rooted for them. I celebrated each tiny achievement: eye contact with someone with autism or someone now able to move a step backward.

The professionals who worked at these facilities were seeing improvements in these participants carrying over outside of the ballroom dance activity time to their everyday lives and functions, which was the goal. This ballroom dance program gave them a voice to feel and express joy through movement, and instead of someone else moving them. This joy was realized through them moving themselves in much more complex actions and interacting socially in an entirely different way. What we take for granted every day in moving our own bodies thousands of times daily or in looking at someone as part of interaction; these individuals may not have previously been afforded the option to move themselves and could not bear to look at someone directly. There is a basic dignity in moving your own body. There is an acknowledgment of the human need to be social and of the want to be interactive by looking at someone directly instead of staying inside oneself – shutting off the outside world. Participants found a way to make their caregivers at the facilities know that they indeed wanted to come to these ballroom dance sessions. The boundaries of neuroplasticity had been stretched. Neuroplasticity is the ability of the brain to form and reorganize synaptic connections, especially in response to learning or experience. New neural pathways were being mapped and used by brains, bones, nervous systems, and muscles so that movements new to them could be done by them!

Where there had been blank faces, emotion now radiated. Not only were social, physical, and mental improvements observed, but feelings surfaced from the inside out. Where there had been primarily instinctive responses from sensations generated outside to inside from someone else touching or moving them, now, in contrast, these feelings and emotions were generated by them or from inside out. Now, they were generating the response based on an emotion felt. Where rooms at geriatric facilities had been quiet, there was now humor, banter, and some healthy competition among seniors regarding their ballroom program.

While my work with those at varying facilities for geriatrics or special needs continued at my own expense, the studio was coming alive. Mirrors were hung, plants were in place, and tables, chairs, and ottomans were positioned. Most importantly, the ballroom music was on with dancers personifying lyrics to a whispering Waltz, teasing Tango, fun Fox Trot or to a cheeky Cha Cha, sultry Salsa, and beckoning Bachata. Clients began to sign contracts for private lessons. Group classes were choreographed. Preparations for competitions were in process. Services and curricula were unfolding. Multi-media marketing was in full swing.

Next came an unexpected opportunity to lead the ballroom dance program at a local university. With this opportunity, several other community events involved my studio. While the studio and university work were classified as for-profit, I saw ways to integrate the studio, university, and non-profit so more could benefit. Since there weren't and still aren't funds to support all of the active non-profit work, I funded such work from the studio starting up. Besides teaching the university students ballroom dancing, I wanted to share with them the values that are important to me. University students were offered positions to be paid to work at the studio and at facilities related to the non-profit programs. While such studio and BD4BU non-profit work were offered to some students, all students involved in the university ballroom dance program were required to be respectful of all always; and to dance with all. Although stating this sounds cold and sterile, in actuality, the students were gentle, kind, inclusive and compassionate beyond expectation. I celebrated them too!

Every cylinder of my being was firing. Yes, I had tons more responsibility and risk, but the stimulation, creativity, and unexpected intangible benefits were making it all worthwhile. The mundane details and issues to be resolved regarding everyday life were all still there of course and magnified more given so many more variables to manage, but, even in greater aggregate, these mundane issues mattered so much less. There was no comparison of my past to my life now as I see someone with special needs do their best to actually run to greet me with such energy and enthusiasm as the anticipation of ballroom dancing inspires them.

While my non-profit volunteer work had started a few years earlier, I had later formally founded the non-profit, Ballroom Dancing For A Better U (BD4BU). By this time, there had been established clients at the ballroom studio, and many of the clients had their own unique reasons for ballroom dancing, whether they realized it or not. Some came to use ballroom dancing as a different kind of therapy to get through a bout of cancer or other illness. Some came to engage in a social activity after a divorce. Others came because it was on a bucket list. The clients were from all walks of life, demographics, and had skills ranging from just trying dancing for the first time to being a seasoned gold-level ballroom dancer. Clients participated in both university events to support the students and contributed as well to support the BD4BU non-profit. A client with a dance teacher background went to facilities with me and the university students employed by my studio to conduct the programs for those with special needs. As there was the integration of people from the studio, university, and non-profit related facilities, lives opened much wider and more wonderfully than could have been imagined. Although dollars needed to be more, the invaluable enrichment of lives happening on all fronts could not be monetized or measured.

As the studio and university programs matured, there were other DWTS local events. One gentleman from our community is a beautiful singer, and he is blind. Seeing one of my university student dance teachers compete with a blind man she had taught to dance for this DWTS event evoked an emotion in the room (and in me) that was palpable. The room went silent with awe and respect watching this student dance teacher, who was a teenager, so lovingly follow this blind man's dance lead. I hosted an equality ball -a ballroom dance competition event, and those with special needs were not only included in the day, but were on the dance floor at the same time with everyone else. Those with special needs were there as equals.

As awards were given out, everyone clapped and was celebrated. One of the special needs participants exclaimed as she received her award certificate: "I did it!" While these three words are easy for us to say, speech, let alone dance, was very difficult for this participant. So to have seen her dance and hear her exclaim with pure joy was marvelous. What is so easy for most of us to do was monumental for her. She has the right to celebrate her achievement and the right to be recognized along with everyone else. Minds expanded, presumptions were dispelled, and hearts melted at that equality ball. As I had mentioned before, I used to silently root for them, but now, silence cannot hold my enthusiasm as I celebrate them out loud!

I have been busier than ever, serving as the advisor for the university ballroom dance club, functioning as the professor leading and teaching the university ballroom dance curricula, owning and administering the studio programs, teaching clients, conducting dance camp weekend programs, running BD4BU, leading the programs at the varying facilities with the participants, and still competing as a professional dancer. Every day is different, darting from one place to the other among university class locations, the studio, and varying facilities where BD4BU programs are happening. I have indeed had more of the opportunities that I was looking for to grow and to create. What I hadn't expected was how much, and in how many different ways I would grow through my own experiences as well as witnessing the growth of many whom I had met.

While altruism can be in the form of a non-profit like, BD4BU, altruism can have additionally substantial and memorable effects in the deeds done just to be kind and to care. Sometimes I hadn't realized this point as I was going about my day until I saw the reaction. The smallest act of kindness can be the key to opening someone up who has been suffering in silence. Caring about the trim on someone's costume, making a quick call, or sending a card can offer so many unexpected rewards. Although this is not a profound revelation, what should not be undervalued is the consequential positive flow of kindness to several or many. One simple act of kindness may be so appreciated by one that that one person can then set into motion a cascading set of good deeds that go on and on.

So, who has time for altruism? I do!

Looking back at my stable life before I took the risk, I would have lived just fine. As a result of taking said risk, I have grown more than imagined and given more than I knew I had. Others have given to me in ways not possibly valued by any currency on the stock market. Living safe and stable is just that – living in a closed-off manner. However, to be alive means to actively and openly welcome the diverse people, experiences, and riches they offer. For every action, there is a reaction, and for every reaction, a cascading series of resulting actions happen as well. While one may never know the details of the infinite resulting impact that goes on and on, just initiating one act of kindness is reason enough to do it.

My wealth will not be measured on Wall Street, but the way I try to live and encourage others to live by giving without expectation can produce a treasure beyond measure.

I am alive, and my life is opened wide.

Danielle Lynn

Danielle Lynn has a true heartfelt passion for helping people of all ages. After recovering from many setbacks in her life (accidents, divorce, bankruptcy, and miscarriages), she felt lost and empty inside. Danielle found happiness by helping others, finding true love, leading with her heart, and regaining self-confidence. Along with an eighteen-year career, she holds a master's degree in social work from the University of Pittsburgh. Danielle is currently working as a drug and alcohol counselor, inspiring adults with her caring demeanor.

Find Danielle online:

Email: 4daniellelynn@gmail.com
Facebook: fb.me/44daniellelynn

Chapter 16

Know Your Worth

By Danielle Lynn

I could not take it anymore. Mentally, physically, and emotionally I felt beaten. I felt destroyed inside. I experienced defeat in life. How could this be? I have always been so strong. I am a social butterfly – smiling and laughing so hard it is difficult to breathe! I have always been told I am that person that lights up a room. Then why was I depressed and so anxious? Why did I begin to isolate myself? My life was completely turned upside down, and I had lost total control. I began to live off salad and wine, and over-exercised daily. My mind and thoughts were all out of sorts, and I remember feeling that I needed to punish myself. I was never one to purposely do any type of harm to myself. I remember thinking, *What am I going to do? What am I doing?*

My life went into a complete transition. I had a miscarriage (possibly twins, I still don't know the truth), lost my ideal job in my career, my husband walked away from our marriage, I lost my home and filed bankruptcy. How many losses can one person experience all at once in a lifetime? This is not normal, right?

A day came where I wanted to shut the entire world out: work, family, friends, and those closest to me. I wanted to be left alone with my pets. I wanted to stay in my house and I began to avoid phone calls. Loved ones were leaving voicemail messages of concern. I remember thinking I wanted the constant chaos in my head to stop. I began to understand what having 'racing thoughts' meant. Everyone's opinions were being thrown at me, and everyone had something different to say. I wondered how my life was such an easy discussion point for everyone else, yet I did not want to discuss anything at all?

One day, I broke. I finally cried. I cried so hard I puked. This had never happened before.

Let me take you back to earlier in the day. I remember having an amazing time at work. On my way home, I called a friend to talk about my day. I got home and began my evening routine of walking on the treadmill, making dinner, taking care of my animals and having a shower. I stepped into the shower, letting the water heat up against my body. I have always enjoyed a hot shower, especially after a busy day. Without thinking, I washed my hair because it is routine. I then grabbed the conditioner. As I did so, I could feel tears filling up in my eyes. I had held these tears in for far too long. My crying turned into an ugly sobbing mess. The next thing I remember is the emotions taking over, kneeling in the shower, crying so hard that my stomach turned into a knot and I began puking. *Where did this come from?* I thought. *I had a good day; no actually, I felt the day was pretty amazing.* After the puking and tears stopped, I sat on the shower floor for what felt like hours.

Never again, is what was in my head, as I sat on the shower floor. Never again will anyone walk all over me. Never again will I doubt myself or think I'm not good enough. Never again will I be financially broke to please someone else. Never again will I say yes to a man because it is 'that' time to be married. Never again will I feel my life depends on someone else. Never again will I feel so alone with my emotions and thoughts and feel taken advantage of. Never again will I feel this way. The next day, I filed for a divorce.

Divorce is not easy and is not cheap. It didn't happen in my family. Today my parents have been married for forty-two years. As their child, I've observed lessons of love, friendship, struggles, and commitment. My divorce took years to finalize, which made it even more difficult to let go. I knew that I never wanted to be with this person ever again, but I had so many different emotions that played on my mind and influenced my actions. I started to map out my life. The counselor in me began to play a role in my life struggles. I wrote down what I wanted for myself out of life, what made me happy, and where I wanted to be. I asked myself, *Who am I?* A lot of my paper was blank. Questions like these are extremely hard when you are true to yourself. I still wanted the typical happy, married life. A life with children and a beautiful home surrounded by family and friends. So basically, a storybook life. Can this really happen? Do many people really have a storybook life?

I was at a point in my life where I needed to work on my emotions and myself. At that moment, I felt like I needed to be alone. As ironic as it was, I still did not make the best choices. I avoided everyone. Family and friends tried to set me up on blind dates, thinking I needed to socialize and get out of my house. But I was not in a place where I felt I was able to meet anyone or even get to know someone. I couldn't have cared less who anyone new was to me. I was a mess; my life was a mess.

It is difficult to be alone. It takes a lot of courage. I had to learn to fall in love with myself again before even thinking about whether someone else could love me again. Often times, people jump right into relationships to avoid their own company. Think of how many people you know that dive into relationships for the wrong reasons. I was not going to be that person. So for months, I was focused on getting *me* back. I meditated, prayed, learned yoga, walked my dogs, cooked new recipes, and began to rebuild a relationship with myself.

Part of making changes within my life and taking control was looking at my finances. Losing my husband's income, my employment, and living off savings meant they were a mess. I had found new employment, but I was living paycheck to paycheck while paying an attorney for a divorce and trying to keep my home. I decided to file for bankruptcy. I had done everything possible to keep my home, but I could not lose any more money. It was not meant to be my home forever. I reconnected with family, family that I knew I kept pushing away for the wrong reasons. I began to live one day at a time. I followed the advice I would give to my own clients in working through life struggles, as a social worker or counselor.

Self-care became a big priority. I wanted to be better and do better, for myself and in life. There are four tips that stand out in my mind that might be beneficial for you, at some point in your life.

1. Know that you are stronger than you think you are!

   I had to dig deep into my emotions and feelings to recognize my strengths and weaknesses. I can honestly say that I know who I am and where I stand in my relationships and with myself. I've learned to be in check with my daily emotions. I used to feel I had this all under control until I experienced my entire life shattering all at once. When you can honestly say you are comfortable with yourself and are able to recognize the obstacles you've overcome, you'll begin to realize how strong you really are. I try to tell people in my personal life and my profession about the power and strength within each of us. I believe it because I have personally experienced this. Your confidence will shine through without being seen as arrogance. If someone disagrees with you on that statement, the issue is more with them than it is about you.

2. Follow your gut!

If something gives you that stomach-turning feeling, then listen. Ask yourself, *Why would I initially feel this way?* I did not follow my gut when I was talking about marriage with my ex-husband. When he asked me to marry him, I was hesitant. It did not seem right to me, but I said yes anyway.

3. Be mindful!

One of the biggest lessons I have learned in life so far is that your words and actions can have a huge effect on other people. Just because you think something in your mind, does not give you the right to speak it. There are too many angry people in our society today. Too many people will push their angry emotions onto others when there is a misunderstanding or disagreement. Talk it out; be considerate of how your feelings may come across to someone else, even while holding your own opinion. Think of your intentions within the discussion. I am not saying be a perfect human being, but be mindful, because words can hurt.

4. Love yourself first!

It is not selfish to love yourself and put yourself first. You are living a life for you. Not everyone will agree with your choices in life, or relationships you may have, but are they healthy choices for *you*? In order to have a better relationship with people you love, you must have a healthy relationship with yourself. So learn what self-care means to you. Look into self-development books, online courses, talk to a professional, whatever it is that helps you. Do not stop educating yourself and learning new hobbies. Always be willing to discover, grow, and learn about yourself.

These four key tips have been an essential part of my life. They helped me to become the woman I am today. I've felt a big shift in my self-confidence during the last few years. I also began to understand the connection with my own thoughts, feelings, emotions, and reactions. Understanding myself better has pushed me further into self-development.

It is also important to understand that self-care is not only beneficial for your own wellbeing, but also for your relationships. Think of it this way, if you do not care about your own needs, it is difficult to care for anyone else's. Every relationship takes continuous work.

Here are three self-care tips for relationships:

1. Take time for yourself!

   This comes back to hobbies, interests, or what makes you happy. The happier and healthier you are, the more fulfilled you will be in your relationships. You will be present for the people that you care about and love.

2. Set healthy boundaries!

   There is an emotional, physical, and psychological space between all human beings and we can sense when they are being violated. Think back to when I spoke about following your gut. It is ok to say no to people you love. Set boundaries and be clear on your needs in the relationship. Your gut and emotions will thank you for it!

3. Get rid of toxic relationships!

    I am still learning that it is ok to let go. Not everyone is meant to be part of your life forever! It does not mean you do not care about these individuals, but maybe they are not meant to be part of your whole story. You might not even realize how toxic some relationships are until they have ended. It is self-care to surround yourself with people that positively impact you and support you, even if they disagree with you. As for relationships that should not and cannot be ended (family members), make sure to set boundaries. I often say, "love people from a distance," so that you can put your needs and life first.

My divorce took years to finalize, and during this time, I realized I could not handle the situation on my own. I was blessed to have family and friends to surround myself with and help sort out my craziness. Even my current husband entered into that hot mess. He still may not realize it, but he is the person that made me feel worthy again. He believed in me, encouraged me to do what I felt was right for myself, supported me emotionally and helped me to believe that I was worth it again. People want to feel loved, important, and to be heard. They want to matter in life. My current husband made me feel all this when I finally said yes to dating him.

I still think of where I am today and how he entered my life while it was in complete chaos. It amazes me how the influence of others plays a role in our lives, good and bad. Love and faith in a partner are what destroyed me. Now love and faith in the right man has brought me back to life. I am back to being that woman that loves life, smiles often, giggles hard, and still finds new hobbies. My life is still a work in progress, and I don't know what my future holds, but I feel stronger, clearer, and healthier.

Coach Reed Maltbie

With master's degrees in both sports psychology and early childhood education, Coach Reed works with youth coaches, helping them teach athletes how to excel beyond the game. Since the release of his 2015 TEDx talk 'Echoes Beyond the Game', he's become a trusted educator, advisor and speaker to sports organizations all over the world.

Coach Reed is a firm believer that youth sport's ultimate role is to develop excellent people with valuable life skills and strong values. He's had the honor of working with sports organizations ranging from grassroots to elite level, helping them become more effective at performance-based communication by building champion cultures, and creating warrior mindsets to succeed in and beyond the game.

Find Coach Reed online:

Websites: http://coachreed.com/
http://changingthegameproject.com
Facebook: https://www.facebook.com/TheCoachReed/
Twitter: https://twitter.com/Coach_Reed

Chapter 17

Chasing Everest

By Coach Reed Maltbie

"The mass of men lead lives of quiet desperation."

- Henry David Thoreau

My wife picked up the phone on the second ring, her voiced was tinged with optimistic anticipation. "How'd it go?"

I paused, contemplating trading the painful truth with a convenient lie. I didn't want to face down the fact that everything I knew was going to evaporate the moment I spoke.

"I think my coaching career is over." I fought the deluge of tears straining for release. I was sitting in the parking lot of my office, watching the sun set across the sky, the metaphor of my career was not lost in this moment. It was unraveling. It was slipping away, and all I could do was watch it drop like a setting sun, destroying another day with red-stained clouds to remind us darkness was descending.

"That bad, huh?" she asked.

I found my voice somewhere amid the racing thoughts. "Worse."

I had coached soccer since I was sixteen years old. I can still recall my coach saying, "This will change your life" when he offered me the chance to work with a local team. He said I had a gift I needed to share, and that this would be a lifelong passion.

Now, as I witnessed the fading light of day, I felt all I had done was fading too. Coaching had given me purpose. It had always been a part of my life, since that day back in 1990. I'd coached soccer for twenty years. It had helped us through tight times, and carried me through tough times. Coaching helped me chase what I believed was my 'Everest' – that one thing that makes other people think we are crazy, but that truly defines us.

The problem with my Everest was the fact it was a part-time job. It was the one thing on this planet I was passionate about, and it was the only 'job' I loved doing. They say do what you love and you'll never work a day in your life. That was coaching for me. I would get up at the crack of dawn, stand in spitting snow, and driving rains to coach a soccer game. It was my happy place. It was where I belonged and where I felt most like myself. It was the reason I was put on this planet.

However, the struggle to follow my purpose was difficult. It didn't pay the bills. I had to keep a day job, which had me pacing my 'cage' like a lion. I wanted to chase my dreams, but I needed to take care of my family.

I was a successful development officer for a very large non-profit organization, high up on the regional flow chart. It was steady, it was safe, and I was paid well. My family was taken care of too. I made enough for all five of us to live well; we had health insurance, retirement plans, and other perks. This was the 'American dream'.

"They told me I have to quit coaching soccer. I have to focus on my day job." My voice was weak, as if saying it softly would lessen the pain it was causing. What we thought was a meeting to offer me a new role with the company ended up being an ultimatum to abandon my dreams.

"No. No. You won't." My wife's voice was loving, firm, and defiant.

My wife was my rock, my greatest supporter. She has never wavered in that role. Whether it was moving several thousand miles for me to 'advance my career', or working a backbreaking jobs so I could chase my dreams, she did it with a reckless abandon. She wanted me to fulfill my 'why', and was willing to make sacrifices for it. It was no surprise she was rattling off the reasons why I could not let my dream die. My mind was flooding with scenarios of what my future in this position would look like without soccer, and she was telling me what it would look like with *more* soccer!

As if she was reading my mind, she paused and then said, matter-of-factly, "I'll tell you what you do. You quit. You quit that job, and chase your dreams. You stop living the life everyone else wants for you. You stop trying to survive so you can be a 'sometimes' coach, and you make it happen. You were put here to transform lives. You can't turn your back on it. You fight for it. You chase it."

That was the exact moment that I stopped trying to survive the world so I could be a part-time chaser of dreams. I had spent my life knowing I was meant to change the world, one youth athlete at a time, but believing I could only do it if I followed the path in the valley.

You see, most of us live those quiet lives of desperation, as Thoreau put it. We follow the path the world prescribes for us, living comfortably, surviving, but desperately wishing we were doing what we knew we were meant to do. Instead of running headlong into our destiny, we stay in the valley of comfort. You know this valley. Where life is relatively easy and placid. We can find all we need to survive right where we live. Sometimes the weather might kick up a little strife, but the terrain doesn't change, and the benefits are all the same. We have our food, our water, our shelter, and our pretty streams to sit by and dream. Life is good (enough), but life is not lived in the valley.

Life is lived on the mountain. Where the terrain changes, and a new adventure awaits every day. Where you wake up every morning driven by a desire to share your gift with the world. Some days are painfully hard on the mountain, unlike the serene valley, but you know you are on your path, chasing your passions and living out your dreams.

Other days are bliss. Not these quiet moments of whispered desperation for something different, but loud, resounding moments of knowing you are doing exactly what you were meant for and wanted to do. That's living!

It is dangerous, terrifying, and uncertain. But it is your path, each day, step by step, along the side of that mountain as you climb for whatever it is you want to climb for, knowing that at the top of that mountain is your destiny. Your 'why'. It is why you were put here, why you do what you do, why you wake up every morning, and why you refuse to ever return to the comfortable valley below. Life may be easier at times in the valley, but it is only a life of survival.

I did end up quitting that night. I stood in that parking lot, staring up at the sunless sky and weighed the balance of my life. It doesn't seem like I should have had such a tough decision, nor does it seem like such a dramatic moment. I wasn't choosing to slay dragons or abandoning my small village in search of truth, or daring the darkest jungles for the lost treasures of life. I was chosen between my dreams and someone else's dreams. Nevertheless, it *was* the most dramatic moment of my life. It was the moment I dared to believe I could chase my Everest and live a fuller life. It was the moment I wondered if life was different on the quest than it was in the comfort of 'wishing' I were on the quest. I chose to stop surviving and opted to start thriving.

Choosing to leave the valley of comfort for the mountain of your dreams is not an easy decision, and it is certainly not an easy journey. It is especially difficult for the ones you love.

Most see the end result and think, *What a beautiful life you lived*, but beneath the surface of it all, I struggled to keep the dream alive. When you make a choice like this, you affect all those who love you and depend on you. My family felt the pain of the journey with me. Whether it was being unable to afford to cover bills until my student loan check arrived, or not taking a single vacation in years because Dad coached year-round in order to make it work, or Mom never being home at night because she was working a second job to keep us afloat. They didn't choose to make the sacrifices; they were simply expected to share in the burden. That weighed on me. To change the world, I had to change the way my family experienced the world too.

I made this choice to chase my Everest and change lives. My family has always supported my mission, but my kids also felt the cruel hand of irony during this journey. When your kids recall you not being at their games because you were off coaching other people's kids, it cuts right to the heart. The burden of knowing the sacrifice my family had to make these last seven years was nearly too much. Climbing the mountain is not easy. Climbing the mountain with the full weight of my families' sacrifice on my back is the hardest thing I have ever done.

In the end, that is maybe the best part of it all – the journey itself. It is never about what you get when you arrive; it is about who you become along the way. For me and for my family, the journey shaped us.

This journey that started in a valley so low I could not see the horizon through all the high buildings, has given me gifts I hope I can pay forward.

I've been given the gift of clarity of vision. The side of the mountain allows one to see further. It allows one to take stock of where they've been and see where they're going. Each day I have clarity about who I am, the gifts I bring to the world, how I can deliver them, and where I am headed. All because I climbed the mountain.

Could I have had clarity in the valley? Maybe, but you can only see so far before something obstructs your view, and you can only dream so much before comfort clouds your thoughts. Even in tough times on my journey, I had clarity about why I was doing what I was doing. It was the clarity that reminded me to keep climbing, and it was the lack of comfort in those tough times that kept the dream vivid. You cannot simply 'lie down to rest a bit' when the going is tough and you know where you are headed. You keep climbing, and you do it with clear eyes.

What is so astounding about the clarity of vision for someone who is choosing to thrive is the contagiousness. When you know without a doubt, who you are, what you are doing, and why you are doing it, others join you without hesitation. What may start as a solo climb becomes a team effort in no time. I always heard, as a child, that the "world gets out of the way for the person who knows where he or she is going". I discovered that actually, the world will join in the climb with the person who knows where he or she is going. My family has climbed alongside me.

The second gift I've received is resolve. When you can see further you, have something for which to strive. You do not give up easily. Fortitude resides in your heart where contentment once lived. You don't want to simply exist. You want to conquer life. The tougher your climb, the more resolved you are to ascend. This fortitude carries you beyond your worst days, days that would have broken you if you were still in the comfort of your valley. The mountain makes you strong.

This resolve also gives rise to hunger. The comfort of the valley means your belly is full and your appetite satiated. During the journey on the mountain, your belly is never full. The fire of knowing you are chasing your Everest never subsides. You hunger for more. Even on 'satisfying' days, the hunger keeps you wanting more. You wake up each morning ready to climb.

What's surprising about resolve is how easy it becomes to continue to shore up on the journey. It doesn't take big days, or epic events to strengthen resolve. It could be something as simple as a phone call from a former player who is now coaching and hopes to have the impact you had, or a text from a former colleague saying, 'Your TEDx made me reconsider how I speak to my athletes'. Those moments propel you rapidly along your journey and steel your resolve.

The final gift that climbing the mountain gives me is an unfettered joy. It may sound strange, given the metaphor of a hard journey as the backdrop, but joy arises from the journey itself. As you see a small, beautiful, delicate flower finding a way to spring forth from between the hardened mountain terrain, you see that joy can arise from it too. That flower had no possible chance of survival on the terrain. It had no way to grow from the rocky ground. It had no sustenance to survive. And yet, there it is, thriving in this unforgiving world. Sharing its beauty with those who take a moment to see it and enjoy it. That flower is joy. One thinks joy is only found in those comforting moments in the valley, but joy exists in every moment on the mountain.

I used to tell my players, "seek joy out there". I knew if they just loved the adventure, had fun in the moment, and did the things that brought them joy, then it would all be worth it. What I never expected, was to find so much joy when I left the valley. Every day brings a new adventure. That adventure itself is joy. Every triumph is joy, every fall makes me feel alive, and every time I realize I am the lucky one because I chose to live the life I wanted I feel unfettered joy.

Joy is so easy to share. When I share my gift with the world, my joy can't be hidden. It's the one thing people remember most. They say I have such passion and joy for what I do, and that, in turn, inspires them. That's the beauty of the gift. That inspires me. The greatest decision I ever made was quitting my day job. That flower rising through the cracks is my Everest extending a small gesture of joy to me for making the right choice.

It's been seven years since that meeting. Where I watched the sun and my dream of coaching fade behind obstacles on the horizon, when I thought survival was my only path. Today, I am above the buildings. I stand at the top of the tallest mountain in San Diego County, looking across all the terrain I have crossed. I'm watching the bright sun dive into the ocean on the horizon, knowing it will come back just as bright tomorrow to light my path. I see all I've accomplished since that night. I see all I still want to do. I know I was meant to do this and I know I have the fortitude and hunger to keep chasing my Everest. This is now our journey now. You and I.

I spot a small flower beaming radiantly among the crushing rocks of the mountaintop. I snap a picture. That flower is my joy: somehow growing on this unforgiving mountain, it is a metaphor of me. Choosing to thrive.

Lisa O'Brien

Lisa O'Brien, E-RYT, CRM is a veteran, certified yoga teacher and was the founder and owner of Bliss Body Studio and Wellness Center from 2004 to 2015. She is a certified Reiki master, as well as an advanced energy intuitive, specializing in clearing blockages and negative programs out of the energy system for healing and advancement on one's path. She developed her empathic and intuitive skills through master teachers, and now specializes in alternative therapies. She offers private and group sessions, as well as teaching meditation, yoga, Reiki, Light Grid, and other energy healing techniques.

Find Lisa online:

Website: www.blissbodynj.com

Chapter 18

Let Go and Let God

By Lisa O'Brien

We are all spirit expressing, observing and beholding to our human experiences. The intention of our individual experiences is to grow and expand on our path to realization, awareness, and enlightenment. I trust my story will inspire others, as others have inspired me. This is my intention for my sharing.

My journey has been filled with desperation, fear, self-doubt, insecurity, and many emotionally charged events. I understand now that for each of these powerful emotions an opposite, positive aspect must exist. With newfound awareness, I choose to tap into my strength, courage, trust, faith and ultimately surrender. There is no wrong way to learn these truths, and like most people, I learn through necessity.

Although all of our journeys begin at birth, this part of mine begins around 1997, where I am a wife and a mother of two children. I have a successful career and a house in a small town where I grew up. I have been working in the same place for over thirteen years with a decent salary, good benefits and accumulated vacation time. From the outside looking in, everything seems like the picture-perfect life of what I dreamed about, but there is something stirring within me, and I am unable to place my finger on it. I have two beautiful boys, but the oldest struggles with ADD and the youngest is struggling with major digestive issues and anxiety. I am frustrated as I have explored many western options of care and they do not seem to be working.

My youngest is in more pain and going deeper into anxiety as time passes. We have been to doctors with many tests and medicines that are only managing the symptoms but not curing the problem. The medical field does not have any other suggestions for us but to keep doing the same things that aren't working.

My relationship with my oldest is becoming more strained as we constantly fight and argue about homework, schoolwork, and everyday matters. I am becoming desperate to help them both and am not sure where to turn. The stirring inside is now screaming at me as my work in the office has become so stressful that I am near my breaking point. A dear friend recommends a book about stress relief through yoga and meditation. It inspires me to pick up a stress-relieving yoga VHS tape and start waking up an hour earlier each day to follow it. It is helping me get to a centered place where I can continue to walk through the office doors and do my job.

A call from the school nurse's office in 2000, with my youngest doubled over in pain and his anxiety escalated, is the final straw. My motherly instincts catapult me into the alternative and holistic field, educating myself in all areas. Reading, attending classes and seminars, and talking with people. I start with holistic nutrition and replace processed and conventional foods with whole, organic ones. There was a bit of a mutiny from the family initially, but in time they settled down, for the most part.

I find myself intuitively placing my hands on my youngest son's head to calm him when he is having an anxiety attack, and it seems to be helping. Being involved with my children's education and outside activities, I volunteer to teach catechism to their age groups and find myself sitting with a Catholic nun, who just so happens to also be a Reiki master, offering to teach me Reiki. My intention is to only offer this to my family and close friends. Little do I know where this is leading.

As I continue to practice yoga with my yoga videos, I explore an actual class where I am inspired to teach yoga to others, and so I enroll in a nine-month two-hundred-hour yoga teacher-training program, and eventually, I continue on to do the advanced training.

Implementing some of the alternative techniques that I have learned, I start seeing improvements in my children, particularly the youngest. It takes less than a year for his digestive system to heal itself, and there is some positive improvement with my oldest as well. The school teachers are asking me what I am doing differently with the boys, so I attempt to get some of these ideas into the school, but old programs die hard, and mindsets are hard to change.

As I continue down this path more doors open, appropriate teachers show up for me to learn, allowing me to grow and expand in this field. I am told I am creating all of this, but I am not quite sure what that really means. I understand it much better now.

Offering the Reiki to my family and close friends expands out to others, and if I am to continue, I need a space to provide the services. I am then presented with an opportunity to rent my own little space, 200 square feet where I can support my small list of clients and teach a very small yoga class. I attempt to continue to work full-time in the office, as well as offer my services of yoga, Reiki, and meditation. This becomes an overwhelming task in balancing family, career and building this new practice of service. I am forced into making a decision about what I'm willing to let go and where I want to place my time and energy.

My family means everything to me, and I truly love and am passionate about offering the holistic work that seems to be really helping others. I am terrified to let go of the full-time stable office job. So I am meditating, praying and praying some more for the 'right' answer. I do not like change when I cannot see where it is leading. I like to know the big picture! With all of this spiritual work, shouldn't I be able to tap into something that will show me the big picture and tell me what to do? Apparently not, and I quickly learn that 'free will' is stronger than anything else. My teachers are telling me that my answers have to come from within. This is initially disappointing. That response is not helping when fear is sabotaging my desires, so I have to learn to let go of the fear and trust in myself and the support of something greater.

I ultimately make the agonizing decision to leave the safe and secure job. There is some turmoil and confusion at the beginning of this transition, as loved ones around me do not understand exactly what is going on. I'm not really sure either, so how can I expect them to understand? I am worried since my income is needed for the household to survive, compounding my fears. It is 2004, so these services are not mainstream in my area. Many people have never even heard of Reiki, and so I am initially labeling it as 'therapeutic touch' as I attempt to explain this ancient form of healing. As for the yoga, this was practiced by 'tree huggers'. I always felt like a bit of a hippy at heart, but now

Compiled by Dana Zarcone

I am told I am taking it to the extreme by getting involved in this woo-woo stuff.

To add to the resistance, the big recession of the economy is taking place, and I am looking to start something new. Bad idea, I am advised, but, something within is nudging and prodding and pushing me to move forward, ignoring all logic and reason.

I am able to save a very small amount of money to sustain me for two months of bills after leaving the office job and focus on my new adventure of offering holistic services full-time. I promise myself to give this new practice 100%, and if things do not grow within two to three years, then I will let it all go and return to my old paradigm. That is how I convince myself to take the leap. Little do I know that once I say yes, there is no going back.

Every fear that can be imagined is arising within me. I know I have to start from the ground and build a reputation with integrity and hard work. This is not something you can really advertise. One cannot just claim to be a good teacher and healer. I know I have to offer more than just my services at my newfound space to sustain the rent. I start teaching at other studios, in colleges, chiropractor offices, churches, wherever someone is inviting me. I also take on a part-time job in a medical office as my guilt programs are firing like crazy in regards to 'bringing home the bacon'. I am just using the phrase, I have taken bacon out of the household meal plans. There is still mutiny around that one from the family.

Once I fully commit to the work, the support of the universe opens doors of opportunity, and I continue learning from master teachers and gaining insights and understandings of my own spirituality. The positive feedback from clients and students is encouraging, and so the work expands and grows. At my five year mark, I need to make a decision to move into a larger space or stay in the status quo.

In 2009, I make the decision to take another chance and expand. A beautiful studio equipped with a gorgeous hardwood floor, mirrors and a decent location is presented to me almost immediately after I say yes to continued growth. I know, without a doubt I am supposed to be there, but it happens so quickly, and I do not have time to integrate it. The next thing I know I am signing papers.

With growth comes growing pains. I begin to experience unexpected rejection. Once owners from outside yoga studios where I am teaching hear of my expansion, they drop me like a hot potato out of fear that I will steal their students. I did not see that coming as the thought never even entered my mind. My illusion that the yoga community is only filled with love and light is shattered for an instant, but the experience helps me understand that human fears are not discerning and show up everywhere and are in everything. It turns out to be a blessing and allows me to focus my energy and time on expanding the work in my new space. It is also a huge lesson that helps me grow on many levels of understanding subconscious programs.

The yoga studio morphs and grows and thrives for the next six years. It is doing well, but requires a tremendous amount of my time and energy to keep it running smoothly. I, gratefully again, find myself at my peak and need to expand or stay in this pattern.

Major changes are taking place in my personal life as well. My children are young adults and creating their own lives, and I am at an impasse where I have to make some major life-altering decisions. My past experiences are helping me with present decisions, as well as using my spiritual tools that I have accumulated over the years. As I release my attachment to the studio, it becomes easier to focus more of my attention on the healing work and discerning where I am out of balance between my personal and professional life. As I begin to feel more balanced, I am able to fully focus on being the facilitator and conduit of the energy work for my clients, and it is being received with many positive results. When fear is removed from the decision-making process, I can then go within where the answers reside.

How do I release fear and the victim programing? I begin by accepting and owning that I am totally responsible for what is going on in my life. I do not blame anyone or anything outside of myself. From this place, I can then make the necessary changes. Since my cells are responding to my belief systems, I need to bring these programs into my awareness where I can then shift them into positive aspects and thoughts. This is how I work with others. Many things run very deep, and it is a continual process that needs to be diligently attended. This is not always easy, but positive changes do take place, and it is worth the effort.

It is our shadow side, that part of self that we do not want to acknowledge exists that is supporting our growth. Without acknowledging it, one might not do their work to remove and release the pain. Attempting to numb it, push it away or ignore it will only manifest into a physical disease that is attempting to get one's attention.

For every negative, there is a positive. This is the law of the universe and manifestation. There is a blessing in every situation, no matter how uncomfortable it may be, if we are able to look deep and hard enough for it.

We are all on this journey together and when we listen to one another's stories,. we can see parts of ourselves in them and learn from the challenges and the triumphs. Be mindful of the difference between listening to a story and attaching to it.

Though most of the formal traditions of storytelling, sitting around the campfire with an elder, is rare these days, it does not mean we have to be without them. It is important to listen to one another, honor one another's journey, and witness the interconnection between every human being.

Today I have a thriving private healing practice and continue to teach yoga and meditation classes as well as other programs. When I created balance in my life in regards to my time, I was offered an opportunity three years ago to host spiritual retreats in Sedona and was able to say yes! They have been very successful, and I look forward to expanding the retreats to other beautiful areas.

I would be negligent if I didn't express my deep gratitude for all of the loving support that I have received from family, friends, teachers, students, clients and many others that are such an instrumental part of my journey. I wouldn't be where I am today without them.

When you create balance and take responsibility for your life and all that is occurring in it, as well as trusting in the process, you will able to let go of fears and be fluid to change. I wake up each morning in gratitude and look forward to my workday and the experiences it holds for me. I am no longer just surviving, I am thriving, and you can too!

Bob Upson

'The Skeptical Pagan' is a lifelong student of world religions and mythology. He has been a minister since 1990 and has a special fondness for weddings between people of diverse religious traditions. His passions include traditional archery, Tang Soo Do, and the value of ritual in human understanding.

Bob is a retired career firefighter now working in the fire sprinkler industry. He holds a Master of Science in Fire Protection Engineering and undergraduate degrees in psychology and fire science technology. He is currently pursuing a master's degree in pagan studies. This chapter represents his first foray into commercially published work.

Find Bob online:

Website: http://TheSkepticalPagan.com
Facebook: https://www.facebook.com/TheSkepticalPagan/

Chapter 19

Knowing When to Walk Away

By Bob Upson

I think I was on duty at the firehouse for every disaster that happened over the last three decades. Two space shuttles, Waco, Oklahoma City, and 9/11, to name a few. I was on morning trash detail in the admin offices when the first plane hit. The Chief kept a TV at his office to watch the morning news so, by the time the second plane hit, we were all watching speechlessly. I don't know how many times I saw that footage over the next few days, but I've never watched it since.

When I returned to school for my master's degree six years later, I found myself studying hundreds of pages of technical reports on the World Trade Center collapses. Over a decade later, there are still changes being made to building codes based on recommendations from those reports. Reports written by my new professors and people who would eventually become my colleagues in fire protection engineering.

Some positive shifts are epiphanies; lightning strokes that come unheralded out of a cloudless sky, leaving change and renewal in their wake. Others happen unnoticed over time; meandering journeys that twist up and down through a landscape of hills and valleys that only reveal in hindsight that we have crossed mountains unaware. My own shift was the latter. I didn't really see it until after I had retired from the fire department and moved on to my second career.

I had been on the job only a little over a year when my first defining incident happened; Thursday, March 5, 1987, a few minutes after noon. It wasn't my regular shift; I was at the firehouse on call-back because both ambulances were out on medical calls. As fate would have it, both returned moments before the fire alarm came in.

In those days, Headquarters was staffed 24/7/365 with four firefighters; the dispatcher and a crew of three for Engine 11. Additional off-duty personnel from Headquarters Company and Engine Company 1 would respond to crew the rest of the apparatus if an alarm came in. We responded immediately with full crews on Engine 11 and Ladder 1. An unparalleled luxury that was still too little too late.

I drove Ladder 1 that day, with my A-shift commander and mentor, 'Scratch' in the officer's seat. He too had come in on a call-back. Our shift commanders carried the rank of 'Paid Lieutenant' because the town manager refused to allow the word 'Chief' in any rank held by a union member. By then I had already known him for a dozen years and had no way of knowing I would only have that privilege for sixteen more. In the end, it was cancer that took him, but it was that day on Center Street that irreparably broke his heart.

We arrived downtown to find smoke and flame belching from the upper floors of a three-story building; a 'taxpayer' with two floors of apartments over a popular deli market. The gathered crowd

171

was frantically reporting children trapped inside. One woman, who had already been removed from the building by off-duty firefighters having lunch nearby, had broken away and run back into the building. She was the only adult fire fatality that day.

As the driver, my job was to position, set-up, and operate the venerable twenty-year-old Maxim truck to access the upper windows and roof with its 85-foot aerial ladder. This involved the hurried but practiced placement of wheel chocks and outriggers to stabilize the truck before mounting the turntable where I'd spend most of the next several hours; delivering firefighters to a third-floor window and, eventually, to the roof after the stairs to the upper floors had been secured. While I set up the truck, Scratch was suiting up and recruiting a partner from among the off-duty firefighters arriving on the scene. The engine crew was already advancing a hose line up the interior stairs against heavy smoke and heat conditions on the second floor. Our task was to get a crew into the third-floor window to search for survivors. Scratch was the first up the ladder.

It was a long time before I learned the details of his search. He injured his ribs climbing through the small window and exhausted his air supply searching in vain for the children we'd been told were somewhere in that part of the building. Crawling in zero visibility, he rolled over and found himself lying on the body of a dead child. Scratch later revealed that he thought his life was over, but he found the resolve to make his way to safety. I remember seeing him later sitting outside in a doorway across from the fire building. I didn't realize that his ribs were the least of his injuries.

By the afternoon's end, four fatalities had been identified, including the young mother, only twenty-five, who ran back into the building in vain for her two-year-old son. Another young mother suffered from cuts and smoke inhalation, but was prevented from re-entering the building where her two sons were lost. It was almost evening before the investigation proceeded to the point where the remains could be removed from the building, and I had my first encounter with an 'if it bleeds it leads' television news reporter who wanted better pictures of the children's bodies for the six o'clock news. It is a wonder that none of the firefighter's carrying the sheet draped litter didn't knock her out then and there.

Scratch gave up his position as a shift commander within a year or two afterward, taking a promotion to a position as our first department training officer. He embraced the new position, but he was never quite the same after the Center Street fire, as it came to be known, and was eventually diagnosed with post traumatic stress disorder (PTSD). His light hadn't gone out, but it never shined as brightly as it once had. He retired in 1993 and finally succumbed to cancer ten years later.

It is only in retrospect that I can really appreciate how this event and its effects on one of my closest friends influenced, not only my fire service career, but also how I dealt with the routine trauma that was 'just part of the job'.

During my early years with the fire department, we operated the town's ambulance service. Some of my most vivid memories involve those ambulance calls. One that stands out came in as a construction accident way across town. Something – it wasn't clear what – had fallen, pinning a worker. We left the station, lights on and siren blaring, for what we knew would be an eight-minute response time at best. Rescue 1 would follow as soon as a crew was assembled. My partner was driving so I was reviewing in my head everything I could remember about industrial accidents and heavy rescue extrication. We could not have been more unprepared for what greeted us upon arrival at the highway construction site.

The worker who met us was strangely quiet and seemed preternaturally calm for an emergency as he led us to the scene of the accident. The 'something' that had fallen was a massive 80-ton steel box-beam destined to support a long span in a new highway overpass. Any thoughts of extrication evaporated instantly. A cable had parted on the massive crane lifting the beam into place, and it had dropped onto the worker below. All that was visible was a bit of the unfortunate victim's brown work boot heel in the scant open space between the beam and the rough wooden pontoon platform it had landed on. That and a single chunk of flesh that had been expelled onto the pontoon a few feet away from the beam. There was nothing to be done for him. I radioed dispatch to cancel the rescue.

We were asked to remain on-scene until an OSHA investigator arrived. It was during that time I noticed the crane operator sitting alone away from the activity, detached and blank. I walked over and sat with him for twenty minutes before we had to leave. Medically, there was not a thing that I could do, but it seemed like it was important to be present for him, at least for a little while. That was the first time I consciously recognized the 'thousand-yard stare' that often accompanies PTSD. I hadn't recognized it in Scratch's eyes back on Center Street when I saw him sitting in that doorway.

Another day, another ambulance call; a welfare check in a grubby little taxpayer building in the wrong part of town. The building manager unlocked the door, but only opened it a crack before we stopped him and shooed him back downstairs. It was summer; it was hot. We didn't need to go any further to know our patient had expired some time before. We came back with air packs to make it official and secure the room for the medical examiner.

He died sitting on the edge of the bed and remained there long enough for rigor to set in before the settling fluids in his body caused his balance to shift, toppling him unceremoniously onto the floor. We found him in a rigid sitting pose but lying face down. A grotesque doll discarded haphazardly on the floor – showing disconcerting signs of bursting in the sweltering heat. The medical examiner eventually arrived, made a perfunctory examination of the deceased, and summoned a car from the coroner's office to bring the departed in for an autopsy.

When the two young coroner's assistants arrived, we suggested that they use our air packs when they went to recover the deceased's remains. They laughed and gave us a hard time about the offer because they were "used to this sort of thing". They made it about halfway up the stairs before coming back out at a trot, both of them a bit green and visibly embarrassed. My partner and I packed up again and took the body bag upstairs to bring him out ourselves. I'll never forget the image of my partner wrapping the deceased's belt around his rigor mortised knees and pulling for all he was worth to get them close enough together to zip up the body bag.

There's a reason firefighters, EMTs, and cops all share the same dark sense of humor. People outside of emergency services sometimes find it offensive. To us, it's therapeutic.

The second defining event in my shift came about two years before I retired. It was in the wee hours of a warm Sunday morning, June 19, 2011, when we were called to a traffic accident on the highway. We had a lot of those with almost 10 miles of interstate running through town. It was an impressive crash, but there was no extrication needed. The ambulances had already departed with their patients before we arrived, but the scene was a mess, two vehicles on their sides blocking all three-travel lanes. Our only real job there was to help clean up any fuel spills and manage the scene until the tow trucks could remove the wreckage so we could open the road. However, that wasn't the event.

By the time the highway was cleared, it was nearing 4 am, and enough traffic had accumulated to be backed up to a complete stop a good half a mile in all three lanes. My truck, Rescue 1, had already been cleared to return to Headquarters and was passing the accident scene in the opposite lane after turning around at the next exit. They would be reopening the highway at any moment. However, as we passed the stopped cars, we realized that there had just been another accident. A car had plowed into the stopped traffic at full speed.

It took a while for us to get to the next exit and loop back. By the time we arrived, another crew had already helped extricate the driver of the last car that had been stopped in traffic before the speeding BMW had rammed it from behind. I had never seen anything like it. The rear wheels of the little Mazda, the whole rear axle and the end of the car attached to it, had been driven forward until they touched the front wheels. The weight of the rolled down windows had been enough to peel the sheet metal skins off the doors on impact. Miraculously, the driver's compartment was intact enough that little extrication was required. She had been loaded into an ambulance with CPR in progress and whisked away to a nearby hospital in almost no time at all. It didn't matter.

Something about that call just stuck in my head. It turned out that the victim was a twenty-two-year-old young lady coming home from her hotel job. That she was well liked, hardworking, and had a plan to move to California. It was all on her Facebook page and the memorial pages set up by her grieving friends. She had just graduated from culinary school and had a bright future, until fate struck in the form of a hurtling juggernaut of German engineering driven by a tired thirty-five-year-old dancer also on her way home from work. One moment of inattentiveness is all it took. After all the calls, all the deaths, all the injuries, this one seemed bizarrely personal.

I don't know when it dawned on me that I had become too obsessed with this incident, but it finally did. By then, over a year later, there were no new posts on the RIP page created by her friends, and the motor vehicle case had already gone to trial. The verdict: negligent homicide with a motor vehicle. Guilty. Six months, suspended, with one year of probation. Somehow, it didn't seem to be enough. Then I remembered. I never met the victim who died, but I did meet the driver of the BMW. If she walked by me tomorrow, I doubt I would recognize her. She was a Latina, attractive I think, but there is one thing I remember clearly. She had the 'thousand-yard stare', and I had completely missed it. Somewhere along the way, I had lost my focus on the living victims and was being drawn down into the same hopeless cycle of fixating on things that cannot be changed. I had wandered onto the desolate slope that had claimed my friend Scratch so long ago. It was time to move on to something different.

My exit plan had been in motion for six years, and I was ready. I had served the time needed to secure my pension. I had prepared myself for a new career, and now it was time to move forward leaving the past behind. After thirty-one years with the fire department, I retired with a clear conscience. I did what I could. I made a difference.

I visit Scratch's resting place from time to time and keep in touch with his family. Sometimes I even manage to toast his memory with the horrid paint thinner that he seemed to think passed for scotch. He taught me a great deal when he was alive. I'll be damned if he isn't still doing it. If you dwell too long on the edge of the pit, it will inevitably draw you in one day. Know when it is time to walk away. The dead are best honored by serving the living.

I still don't watch movies about 9/11 and have still never brought myself to visit the site. Ironically, I finally saw it from the air a couple of years ago returning from a business trip on 9/11. It's time to go and pay my respects to those who were lost and homage to those who survived.

Conclusion

So, there you have it! Inspiring stories from amazing people who shifted from simply surviving in their lives to totally thriving. I'm very proud of every author that contributed to this book. Their shifts have been nothing short of amazing!

They exposed their vulnerabilities so you can learn from their experiences. Some of these authors revealed parts of themselves they've never shown before. In part, it was because they knew that it would help them in their own healing process, but mostly because they wanted to inspire you, the reader.

They wanted to show you that we *all* go through really tough, challenging times. It's not the challenging times that matter, it's the lessons we learn along the way. Like the authors, you won't be given anything you can't handle.

It is my hope that you found a little bit of yourself in each of these stories and you realize that you, too, can move from surviving to thriving. If you're suffering in some area of your life, there's nothing to be ashamed of, and there's nothing to fear. You can make that change. You've got this!

If you enjoyed this book, we'd all appreciate it if you'd hop on over to Amazon and write a review. This way the authors will know they did – indeed - have an impact! Thank you in advance for your support on this journey.

Remember, at the end of the day, in order to live your life all-in and full-out, *Your Shift Matters*.

Dana Zarcone,
The Liberating Leadership Coach.
Coach I Trainer I Best Selling Author I Publisher I Motivational Speaker
www.danazarcone.com

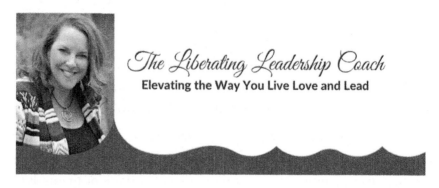

The Liberating Leadership Coach
Elevating the Way You Live Love and Lead

You are a leader! You may be leading a company, organization or team. Or maybe you're leading a little league, Girl Scout troop, Bible study or a PTO. Either way, you are a leader! The question then is, are you a good leader?

Maybe you're a passionate, intelligent person, but you're feeling stuck, frustrated, stressed, depressed or overwhelmed? Perhaps you're a manager who is having trouble motivating your team and, as a result, morale is low while absenteeism and presenteeism are at an all-time high. Maybe you're a healer, coach, author, speaker or coach that is paralyzed by procrastination, lack of confidence and self-doubt.

Step into your role as a leader with courage, confidence, and clarity!

Dana integrates neuroscience, quantum physics, kinesiology, and psychology to show her clients what is truly possible.

She helps them to:

- Shift from a manager to a leader / leader-developer
- Build a motivated, passionate team
- Boost morale – yours and your teams
- Build a successful coaching or speaking business
- Minimize stress and optimize mental health

If you're ready to elevate the way you live, love and lead visit www.DanaZarcone.com today!

CPSIA information can be obtained
at www.ICGtesting.com
Printed in the USA
BVOW09s2120150318

510729BV00015B/174/P